The Peace Corps

KINDLERS OF THE SPARK

The Peace Corps

KINDLERS OF THE SPARK

by Edna McGuire

Introduction by Donovan V. McClure
Associate Director, Office of
Public Affairs, The Peace Corps

THE MACMILLAN COMPANY, NEW YORK
COLLIER-MACMILLAN LIMITED, LONDON

¿ 72 219

The Macmillan Company, New York
Collier-Macmillan Canada, Ltd., Toronto, Ontario
Library of Congress catalog card number: 66-10697
Map by William Metzig
All photographs courtesy the Peace Corps
Printed in the United States of America
Second Printing, 1967

Introduction

In the late summer of 1961, forty-nine American teachers deplaned at the West African port of Accra. Within a week they had become part of Ghana's national school system, and the first implementers of America's idea for a pragmatic, practical alternative to war: the Peace Corps.

The arrival of those first volunteers happened behind the tension of crossed fingers in America. There were skeptics who, recalling Clemenceau's adage, "War is much too serious a matter to be entrusted to the generals," believed peace was too tenuous to be committed into college boys' hands. Yet only four months later three of these volunteers were elected assistant principal, or principal, of their assigned schools. (How frequently do today's Africans elect white men to positions of authority?)

Now, four years later, the Peace Corps is at work in forty-six nations of Asia, Africa and Latin America. Almost 14,000 volunteers are teaching school, building bridges, soldering pipes, coaching basketball, and teaching by example the thousand and one chores that go into the development of viable, democratic economies.

The broad concept of the Peace Corps is that unequal standards of living among nations are an intrinsic cause of war. Consequently, by helping developing nations improve their material circumstances the cause of peace is furthered.

As Peace Corps volunteers bring Western technical know-how to developing nations, they are at the same time giving the people a new awareness of individuality, of personal dignity. So the Peace Corps attack upon war is twofold: economic and humanitarian.

This is the grand strategy, and grand strategems are achieved by little sorties. Peace Corps volunteer Judy Conway of Boone, Iowa, served in the Philippines. Taking the unused portion of sugar cane, she attached the fuzz of a local plant and came up with paint brushes for her students. Then she made paints from local plant dyes and opened an art school in her village.

Judy also started a local industry. Again using sugar cane, she designed and wove mats. The villagers followed her example and the mats became best sellers in a number of Philippine communities.

This is the kind of ingenuity and initiative that we expect of Peace Corps volunteers. They aren't ten feet tall, they aren't miracle workers in the mystic sense, and they probably won't see dramatic results from their two-year stays in foreign lands. But their footprints are indelible. Every country hosting volunteers has requested double and even quadruple the original number.

In her research for *The Peace Corps: Kindlers of the Spark,* Edna McGuire has done a great deal more than collect statistics. She has met, talked with, and experienced a bit of the life of Peace Corps volunteers. She hasn't experienced it all, of course: the boredom, the frustration, the loneliness, the thrill of the little wins that will perhaps in time add up to success in the grand strategy.

But she has caught the spirit of Peace Corps *motivation*—that *x* reason why volunteers care—whether a Peruvian slum child learns to read or not; whether a bridge is built to span a little-known river in Tanzania; care *enough* to accept perhaps a two-year handicap in the competition of living back home.

The goal of developing countries is not just better dams, better hospitals, or better highways. The goal is better people. And this is the goal, too, of the Peace Corps.

The Peace Corps is, in the words of Alberto Lleras Camargo, former president of Colombia: "The finest way in which the

United States could prove to the humble people of this and other lands that the primary purpose of its international aid program is to build a better life in all of the free world's villages and neighborhoods."

There can be no higher national purpose.

Donovan V. McClure
Associate Director
Office of Public Affairs
The Peace Corps

To Peace Corps volunteers, who through dedicated service have helped people the world around to acquire new skills, to develop changed attitudes, to achieve a sense of personal dignity, and to set for themselves worthy goals

I wish to acknowledge with deep gratitude the assistance and cooperation which I received from many people while doing research for this book. I am particularly indebted to the Peace Corps volunteers and to members of the Peace Corps staff who shared their experiences and upon occasion their homes with my husband and me as we journeyed around the world to secure firsthand knowledge of the Peace Corps in action.

Edna McGuire

Contents

By Way of Explanation

This is the story of a pilgrimage made to see the Peace Corps in action. In 1961 the Peace Corps was only an idea. Today it is a people-helping-people program in forty-six countries spread around the earth. The actors in this far-flung pageant of service are the Peace Corps volunteers—many of them young, some in the middle years, a few older, but all Americans far from home. No one of them alone will change the course of history, but the world is a different place because they serve, for they have brought skills to the unskilled, friendship to the friendless, hope to the hopeless.

To tell a story of the volunteers based upon firsthand knowledge meant traveling to the lands where the volunteers were on duty, seeing their projects, talking with them, meeting the native people with whom they worked. Since it was impossible to travel to all the countries, five countries were selected to be visited. These countries were chosen to provide geographical spread, cultural diversity, and a wide range of Peace Corps activities. They included Ecuador in South America, Sierra Leone and Tunisia in Africa, India and Malaysia in Asia.

My husband and I spent three months traveling in the selected countries. It was not possible for us to visit every volunteer working in these countries, but one hundred forty volunteers generously shared their experiences and often their houses with us. Busy Peace Corps executives arranged schedules for us, offered advice, and extended hospitality. Local people helped further understanding of their countries, spoke their praise of volunteers, and upon occasion invited us to their homes.

These pages offer the record of some of the observations that we made, some of the conversations that we held. In the limits of one book it is not possible to mention every volunteer interviewed or to relate every experience encountered, though selecting from the wealth of material acquired on the journey was difficult. However, we here record our gratitude to each and every volunteer and to all other persons who helped to make our trip to three continents a memorable experience.

This, then, is the story of the journey which we made when we flew around the world to see an idea in action. Through the action here portrayed in five countries, we hope that the reader may better understand the purposes and achievements of America's Peace Corps volunteers, who serve as kindlers of the spark.

Edna McGuire

1. THIS IS THE PEACE CORPS

The Power of an Idea

A tall, blond girl entered a hospital convalescent cottage in India. The girl was an American nurse. The patients in the cottage, all Tibetan men, were refugees who had fled their country when it fell to the Communist Chinese.

Smiles lighted the faces of the patients when they saw their visitor. Their chatter ceased. The checker game played by four men sitting cross-legged on a bed was abandoned.

The Tibetans lifted their hands held palm to palm in the Indian gesture of welcome, known as *namaste*. They called greetings in Tibetan to the girl and some, bolder than others, tried a second greeting in English. Their mastery of the new tongue was less than perfect, but their intention to compliment their American friend was evident. Dorothy Nyberg, Peace Corps volunteer, returned the compliment by replying in her best Tibetan. Smiles dissolved into chuckles that registered appreciation of the nurse's effort.

This day of the nurse's visit was a very special holiday in India. All over the country illuminations had been prepared for lighting. When darkness fell myriads of flickering candles and the flaming roar of rockets would proclaim that this was Diwali, the Festival of Lights. Dorothy Nyberg had chosen her own means of honoring the day and the country in which she served. She had for this occasion laid aside her white nurse's uniform and donned an Indian sari. As she moved between the beds speaking to the men, checking charts and giving instructions, the graceful folds of the sari floating about her served in a sense as a banner of goodwill.

Leaving the cottage of the Tibetans, Dorothy continued on

her rounds. She was eagerly welcomed in each cottage. The Indian men, like the Tibetan men, had warm smiles for their friend. But the Indian women had an even closer bond. They had donned their best saris in honor of Diwali and when they saw Dorothy, also in a sari, they accepted her as one of their own. Crowding about her, they touched the garment, with little cries of approval. Dorothy admired each woman's sari and complimented the wearer on her appearance. At the nurse's words the faces of the Indian women lighted up like Diwali candles.

It was a small Tibetan girl, however, who gave voice to the deep feeling of the patients. When five-year-old Dewa saw her good friend Dorothy Nyberg enter her cottage she ran to the nurse and threw her arms around Dorothy's knees. With her head pressed tightly against the folds of the nurse's sari, Dewa cried, "I want to go with you! I want to go with you!"

This hour in which Dorothy Nyberg went about her duties at the Madar Union Sanitorium had within it all the elements that make the American Peace Corps a successful service organization in underdeveloped countries. It was the Peace Corps in microcosm. Here was a Peace Corps volunteer who was sympathetic with the culture of the country in which she served, who cared about the people with whom she worked, and who identified with their hopes and interests. Because the people sensed these qualities in the volunteer they accepted her as one of their own and gave her loyal devotion. And because the volunteer and the people had established good rapport they found mutual happiness in their relationship.

The Peace Corps is people working with people. The volunteers go to help other countries develop the skills and techniques which will enable them to improve the living conditions of their people and build stronger economies. To do this, volunteers must do more than merely teach new skills and techniques. They must inspire the people with whom they work to want to solve their own problems. To kindle the spark of inspiration may well be the most important work of a Peace Corps volunteer, but this can be achieved only if there is mutual respect and understanding. Dorothy Nyberg, nursing tubercular patients in a mission hospital near Ajmer, India, is one of several thousand Peace Corps volunteers who have gone out hoping to serve as kindlers of the spark.

The Peace Corps is an idea turned into action.

The idea is not new. For more than a hundred years men toyed with the thought of the good that might be done by a force dedicated solely to improving living and working conditions. Churches and other organized groups acted upon the idea and their efforts were useful. But as people burst the bonds of colonialism and scores of new nations emerged, the need for new skills and modern techniques increased tremendously.

Proposals to establish a corps of American volunteers to serve in underdeveloped countries were made both in and out of Congress. For a time these proposals received scant attention. The idea was triggered into action in September 1960, when Senator John F. Kennedy called for the establishment of a "peace corps." Senator Kennedy, then a candidate for President of the United States, was elected to the presidency in November 1960.

Soon after President Kennedy took office in 1961, he set about the creation of a Peace Corps. One of his first actions was to appoint Sargent Shriver the director of the Corps. In response to his appointment the director made the President a promise. "Mr. President," Shriver said, "this could be the worst boondoggle in history or a real going outfit. I'll try to make it a going outfit."

Sargent Shriver enlisted the help of a group of people who were interested in the type of program that he hoped to establish. This group met day after day all through February 1961, in a Washington, D.C., hotel room. They proposed plans and tore them to pieces. They agreed upon some points and argued over others. They knew they had, as Shriver put it, "a great, fine, beautiful idea." Their difficulty was to determine how to turn the idea into a practical program.

A month of agonized discussion and argument produced a plan of action, which Sargent Shriver submitted to President Kennedy. The President accepted the proposed program and on March 1, 1961, issued an order that established the Peace Corps on a trial basis, with the hope that Congress would establish it on a permanent basis.

Again, Sargent Shriver had work to do. This time he had to persuade members of Congress that the Peace Corps should be authorized by law. This was a task for which the Peace Corps director was well suited, for he is a man who combines enthusiasm for ideas and ideals with respect for the practical means by which they must be turned into action.

The President asked the Vice-President, Lyndon B. Johnson, to head a council of Peace Corps advisors. The Vice-President, who had had years of experience as a member of Congress, lent his knowledge and energy to the task of shaping the Peace Corps into a workable organization and securing Congressional approval. The supporters of the idea were successful. On September 22, 1961, the Congress of the United States established the Peace Corps by legislative action, and provided an appropriation of money to support it.

The purposes of the Peace Corps, defined in the law, were:
1. To help the people of interested countries meet their needs for trained manpower;
2. To help promote a better understanding of the American people on the part of the people served;
3. To help promote a better understanding of other peoples on the part of the American people.

The plan for the new Peace Corps was commended by many

Americans but condemned by some. Those who believed in the Corps used such terms of praise as "a happy inspiration" and "an inspired American experiment." Those people who doubted that the Peace Corps could succeed hailed it as "Kennedy's Kiddie Corps" and "a Crewcut Crusade."

The Communist countries raised a great clamor, calling the Peace Corps "a super-spy organization." Even some people abroad who were friendly to the United States doubted that the Peace Corps could succeed. One official of a foreign government spoke his doubts to Sargent Shriver. Recalling the beginning of the United States, this man said, "Yours was the first revolution, but do you really think your young people possess enough of this revolutionary spirit to respond to your Peace Corps?"

"Yes," was Sargent Shriver's crisp reply.

Some foreign leaders expressed their surprise that this idea of unselfish service had blossomed into reality in the United States. The King of Thailand said, "The Peace Corps volunteers have shown us a whole new side of the United States." The Foreign Minister of Thailand went even further. He said, "It is indeed striking that this important idea, the most powerful idea of recent times . . . should come from the mightiest nation on earth, the United States. Many of us who did not know about the United States thought of this great nation as a wealthy nation, a powerful nation . . . But how many of us know that in the United States ideas and ideals are also powerful?"

Who, Where, What, and How

It was a scorching hot July day in the Missouri Ozarks, but Camp Cloverpoint was a buzz of activity. Two men lugged stones to a tree-shaded spot, while a third man, on his knees, fitted the stones in place to form a crude oven. Nearby another group of men were lashing rough boards together with heavy twine in the hope of producing a table. A half-dozen girls labored over a kettle set on three stones, filling the kettle with water, feeding the fire under the kettle with sticks, and watching for the water to boil.

Cries of consternation came from the young men and women gathered at a little distance for a lesson in killing and dressing chickens. Faces were averted and protests were voiced as the instructor, armed with a sharp butcher knife, showed the girls how to cut off a chicken's head.

"I can't do that," a young woman moaned. "I simply can't!"

But she did it, nevertheless, when her turn came. And summoning her courage, she continued preparations for dinner by plunging the fresh-killed chicken into a pail of hot water dipped from the bubbling kettle. A young man joined her and together they gingerly plucked at the hot, wet feathers. When a bunch of feathers came off, the girl, with a gasp of surprise, exclaimed, "Look, it really does work! The feathers come off!"

Preparations for dinner moved forward. The chickens, suspended from spits over a fire, roasted to mouth-watering crispness; corn secured at a near-by farm boiled in the kettle; biscuits baked in the homemade oven. When the eighty campers gathered for the meal, they ate with appetites born of hard labor, but the satisfaction they felt was more than appreciation

Peace Corps volunteers bound for the Far East receive instruction in dressing chickens at the advanced training camp in Hawaii.

of good food. They also experienced the satisfaction of knowing that they could obtain and prepare their food without the aid of modern conveniences.

The young men and women gathered for a week's stay at Camp Cloverpoint were not there merely for an outing. They were Peace Corps trainees having firsthand experience with some problems of primitive living which they could expect to meet when they reached their assignments in Ecuador. They had begun their training in mid-June on the campus of the University of Missouri at Columbia. The week of camping in late July would be followed by another month on the campus.

Many of the trainees, when they became volunteers in Ecuador, were scheduled to serve and live in villages where there were few, if any, conveniences. The skills they learned at Camp

Cloverpoint would be useful for their own survival as members of a village community. Moreover, their ability to perform successfully the simple chores of which the Ecuadorians were masters would win for them the respect of the native people.

The trainees at Camp Cloverpoint did more than learn to prepare their own food. They learned to purify their water, either by boiling or by the use of chemicals, a precaution that they must use in most of the cities of Ecuador as well as in rural areas. They learned to make soap. They dug irrigation and drainage channels. They worked at building and grading roads. They learned how to pick a good horse, because some of them would have to use horses to reach mountain villages not served by public buses.

The trainees had little familiarity with farm life so they were loaded into buses and taken to visit Missouri farms. There they learned something about the growing and harvesting of grains. They saw the methods used in raising cattle, sheep, hogs, and poultry. They exclaimed over the charms of new-born pigs. And they learned a healthy respect for the achievements of men and women who day in and day out draw a living from the land.

The trainees at the camp took long hikes to test their endurance and improve their physical condition. They used their Spanish in daily conversation. They continued to explore facts and ideas presented in their campus training.

Camp Cloverpoint, on the east shore of the Lake of the Ozarks, is linked to the main highway only by a dusty country road. It is an isolated place and for that reason more useful as a training center. Yet in one sense this woodsy spot in the Missouri Ozarks is not in the least isolated, because it has provided an essential part of the training for America's most successful ambassadors to other lands. Skill in plucking a chicken, acquired by a trainee at Camp Cloverpoint in the Ozarks, could prove to be the open sesame for a volunteer in an Indian village in the Andes.

Sargent Shriver and his fellow workers who determined policy for the newly created Peace Corps faced certain basic questions, to which they had to find immediate answers:

Who could serve as a Peace Corps volunteer?

Where would volunteers go?

What would volunteers do?

How would volunteers be selected?

How would volunteers be trained?

All qualified, single Americans above eighteen years of age were invited to join the Peace Corps. So were married couples with no dependents under eighteen, if both could qualify for the same project. It was decided that volunteers would receive a modest cost-of-living allowance while in service and at the end of their tour of duty an amount equal to seventy-five dollars for each month of service. In response to the invitation to join the Peace Corps more than a hundred thousand Americans have applied for service and over fourteen thousand have served in the Corps. Most volunteers are young people, but a number are past sixty years of age and a few are past seventy. Both single people and married couples have responded to the call.

It was decided that the Peace Corps would go only where invited. Invitations poured into the Peace Corps Office from countries desiring to upgrade skills and improve the living conditions of their workers. Volunteers have served in forty-eight countries, but have been withdrawn from Cyprus and Indonesia because of internal conditions in these two nations. Other countries who have requested help are on the Peace Corps waiting list. The map on pages 42-43 shows the countries where volunteers were serving in September 1965.

Volunteers must be "doers," not "advisers." This statement from policy makers set the pattern for Peace Corps service, but it left unanswered the question, "Exactly what are volunteers to do?" Experience showed that the answer was, "Whatever needs to be done."

Nearly all volunteers add a second, and sometimes several, assignments to their basic assignment because they see so much that needs to be done. Peter and Rosalie Williams, for example, were teachers in Sierra Leone, but they also promoted poultry raising and gardening and were the moving force in digging wells and in building and equipping a library in their town. Peace Corps volunteers are not only doers but flexible doers.

The greatest demand in underdeveloped countries is for teachers—at all levels and in all subjects, but especially teachers of mathematics and science. Almost as great is the demand for volunteers who can improve farming practices. But the list is endless. Skilled craftsmen, professionally trained persons, and volunteers without a skill, but capable of mastering one, are all urgently needed. The chart on pages 24-25 shows the types of work in which Peace Corps volunteers were engaged as of June 1965.

Colombia trainees dig a cistern in a village near Taos, New Mexico.

Peace Corps Volunteers

| AREA | AGRI. EXT. | COMM. DEV.—RURAL | COMM. DEV.—URBAN | EDUCATION | | | | | | HEALTH | MULTI-PURPOSE | PUB. WORKS | LAWYERS | PUB. ADMIN. |
				ELEM.	SEC.	UNIV.	ADULT	VOC.	PHYS.					
AFRICA														
Cameroon		✔			✔									✔
Ethiopia				✔	✔	✔		✔		✔			✔	
Gabon		✔			✔			✔				✔		
Ghana			✔		✔							✔		
Guinea	✔				✔									
Ivory Coast					✔		✔		✔					
Kenya		✔			✔									
Liberia				✔	✔			✔					✔	✔
Malawi		✔		✔	✔					✔				
Morocco		✔			✔				✔	✔				
Niger	✔						✔			✔				
Nigeria	✔	✔			✔								✔	
Senegal		✔	✔					✔						✔
Sierra Leone		✔			✔								✔	
Somalia					✔									
Tanganyika	✔			✔	✔					✔		✔		
Togo	✔				✔					✔				
Tunisia	✔				✔					✔		✔		
Uganda					✔									
ASIA & FAR EAST														
Afghanistan					✔			✔		✔	✔	✔		✔
India	✔	✔	✔		✔			✔		✔				
Iran	✔	✔			✔	✔		✔						
Malaysia		✔	✔	✔	✔	✔		✔		✔				

by Category of Programs

AREA	AGRI. EXT.	COMM. DEV.—RURAL	COMM. DEV.—URBAN	EDUCATION — ELEM.	SEC.	UNIV.	ADULT	VOC.	PHYS.	HEALTH	MULTI-PURPOSE	PUB. WORKS	LAWYERS	PUB. ADMIN.
ASIA & FAR EAST cont.														
Nepal	✔	✔			✔	✔								
Pakistan	✔	✔			✔					✔		✔		
Philippines				✔	✔	✔	✔							
Thailand		✔			✔	✔				✔				
Turkey	✔	✔	✔		✔			✔		✔				
LATIN AMERICA														
Barbados					✔									
Bolivia	✔	✔				✔				✔				✔
Brazil	✔	✔	✔		✔	✔				✔				
Br. Honduras		✔		✔	✔			✔						
Chile	✔	✔	✔			✔		✔		✔				
Colombia	✔	✔	✔	✔	✔	✔		✔	✔	✔				
Costa Rica		✔				✔				✔				✔
Dom. Rep.	✔	✔	✔							✔				
Ecuador	✔	✔	✔		✔	✔		✔	✔			✔		
El Salvador	✔	✔				✔								
Guatemala	✔	✔				✔								✔
Honduras		✔	✔			✔				✔				✔
Jamaica				✔	✔	✔		✔	✔					✔
Panama	✔	✔	✔			✔				✔				
Peru	✔	✔	✔		✔	✔		✔		✔				
St. Lucia				✔				✔						
Uruguay	✔		✔											
Venezuela		✔	✔			✔	✔		✔					

Based on Peace Corps statistical summary of June 30, 1965

Peace Corps volunteers are selected on merit. A person interested in volunteering fills out a lengthy application form or questionnaire. Letters concerning his ability are secured from six persons whose names he has listed as references. He takes a test. The questionnaire, letters of recommendation, and test results are studied by Peace Corps officials. If they feel that the candidate has the qualities necessary to become a successful volunteer, he is invited to train for the area of the world for which he has expressed a preference on his application. During training the Civil Service Commission makes a background check of the candidate for security reasons. Final selection is made at the end of the training period.

Three requirements are made of the candidate. He must be in good physical condition. He must have personal traits that seem to promise success. By the end of his training he must have skills that match the technical requirements of the job to be performed overseas.

When a candidate is accepted for training he usually reports for a ten- or twelve-week training session on a college or university campus, though occasionally at a private agency instead. Training with him are other candidates going to the same country to which he is going.

Tough days are ahead for the trainee. He will be expected to study at least sixty hours each week. He will often need to learn one of the international languages and nearly always a local or tribal language as well, for experience has shown that mastery of languages is a volunteer's greatest advantage. The trainee must delve into the history, geography, culture, and customs of the country to which he expects to go. He will review the history and traditions of the United States in order to interpret America to other people. He will sharpen his own skills and learn how best to use them in the country where he will serve. He will engage in strenuous physical exercises—running, jumping, swimming, weight-lifting, and others. Sometimes, as was the case with the trainees at Camp Cloverpoint, he will inter-

An Ecuador trainee tests his fitness and endurance.

rupt his campus training in order to develop basic living skills.

Volunteers who have completed service in the country for which a group is training often join the university instructors in preparing the trainees for their work abroad. These experienced volunteers explain conditions in the host country to the candidates. They warn of problems that trainees will meet. They discourage the fond dream of many trainees, that they will work miracles of improvement in the areas where they work. But even while these experienced volunteers try to reduce expectations to realistic proportions they also strive to keep alive the enthusiasm and interest of the trainees, for they know that a successful volunteer must neither expect too much nor care too little.

The trainee who survives his first training may be sent to one of several Peace Corps camps or centers for advanced training and field work. Such advanced training sites have been established in New Mexico, Hawaii, Puerto Rico, and the Virgin Islands. Certain trainees receive field training in neighboring countries. Some who are bound for French-speaking countries go to Quebec, Canada, and others, who are going to Latin America, train in Mexico.

Advanced training camps and centers offer a sample of life as the volunteer will find it on his job. The trainees live in primitive quarters, which in some cases they build. They secure their own food in gardens, fields, and markets. They butcher their meat and cook it over open fires or on primitive stoves. In all camps trainees do field work. In Puerto Rico this may involve helping to advance the island's famous community development program, known locally as community education. In New Mexico the trainees work in Indian villages which have some of the same problems they will meet in the Indian villages of Latin America. In Hawaii trainees may learn to plow with a water buffalo, to plant and care for tropical crops, to build a bamboo house, or to thatch a roof.

In the Peace Corps camps trainees receive physical and psychological conditioning. They are asked to undertake severe physical exercises such as scaling a rock wall with climbing ropes. As a trainee hangs suspended on the face of the rock, he discovers that he must summon all his strength and self-confidence to succeed. The purpose of this exercise is to challenge the trainee to uncover his hidden reserves.

Orientation in the country where the volunteer serves is the last stage of training. In these final days the volunteer comes face to face with the language he must speak, the customs he must observe, the tasks he must perform. In meeting these new situations the volunteer knows moments of uncertainty, but he is sustained by his hard-earned experience in training.

The Way They Live

Bob Agro and Bill Vickers, Peace Corps volunteers in Ecuador, established a snug home in a round grass hut. The hut stood on the high plains at the foot of Mt. Cotopaxi, a snow-crowned volcano rising twenty thousand feet high. Around the hut of the volunteers were similar huts occupied by the eighty-six Indian families of San Augustin de Callo.

Each hut, or *choza*, was fashioned by covering a wooden framework with thick layers of the tall grass that grows on the plains. The hut had no windows but the wooden door, standing open much of the time, admitted light and air.

Bob and Bill furnished their choza with two cots, a table, several stools, and the shelves of books provided to volunteers by the Peace Corps. A two-burner gasoline stove for cooking and a gasoline lantern supplied by the Peace Corps were luxury items in an Indian village. Bob and Bill's pet dog added a cozy touch of home to the household.

The Indians had never seen a white man living in a choza. At first they were surprised and curious, but they were soon on good terms with the volunteers and making daily visits to their hut.

One evening when Bob and Bill had an important Peace Corps guest the Indians decided to help entertain the visitor with a little joke. The man was seated on a stool near the wall of the hut. Suddenly the shining blade of a machete pierced the grass wall and flashed past the visitor's elbow. With a yell, the man was off the stool and across the hut in one leap. The sounds of muffled laughter outside told Bob and Bill that their Indian friends had paid them another visit.

Jim Samiljan, volunteer in Ecuador, worked at community development in one of Guayaquil's worst slums. He was unable to find a room in the bamboo shacks of this slum so he rented an upstairs apartment on a nearby street. The apartment, which had three rooms and a bath, cost Jim the equivalent in Ecuadorian money of twelve dollars a month. This modest rent pleased him. The only flaw was the lack of water in the bathroom. But water was available at the first-floor level and Jim was ingenious, so he solved that problem—almost. He placed barrels on the roof with pipes leading to the two bathrooms in the building and bought a handpump. Patient pumping filled the barrels. At the turn of a handle the shower flowed and the toilet flushed.

Jim reflected upon the ease with which a Peace Corps volunteer can solve his problems. But his reflections were cut short by the sound of splashing water and a chorus of giggles. The noise was coming through the thin partition that separated his landlord's bathroom from his own. Apparently, the landlord's teen-age daughters were enjoying a shower. Jim rushed to his own bathroom, only to find his fears confirmed. When he opened the faucet in his shower not a drop of water came.

Jim tried again, laboring over the pump. But no sooner were the barrels filled than the landlord's family indulged in the luxury of showers. Repeated experience taught Jim the wisdom of lugging buckets of water into his bathroom instead of filling the barrels on the roof. He used the water in the buckets to splash himself in the shower.

"I have the plushest assignment in India. This is a good school. I teach in English. The boys are eager to learn. And look at this comfortable apartment. It even has an American-style bathroom!" The speaker was Henry Gwiazda, a Peace Corps teacher at the secondary level in the Methodist Boys School in Hyderabad, India.

Mary Ann Lawrie, usually called Toni, Peace Corps volunteer and head nurse in the Sri Menanti Rural Health Sub-Center in Malaysia, lived in a house provided by the Rural Health Service. Like other Sub-Center nurses' quarters in Malaysia, Toni's house had a pleasant living room, two bedrooms, a dining room, kitchen, and store room. There was also a walled, floored patio and bath facilities. The comfortable furnishings included a kerosene-burning refrigerator. When the Sub-Center Clinic was open for patients, the generator provided electricity for Toni's house, as well as for the Clinic.

These experiences of volunteers indicate a wide variation in living conditions. Some volunteers live in primitive housing and experience physical hardships. On the other hand many volunteers, like Henry and Toni, live in comfortable quarters and suffer few inconveniences.

The Peace Corps expects a volunteer to live in the community in which he works, in order that he may identify with the people and understand their problems. The Corps also expects that, as far as possible, the volunteer will live on the same level as natives of the host country who are doing the same type of work performed by the volunteer.

Visitors are a part of every volunteer's daily life. His callers are old, young, and all the in-between ages. They may arrive uninvited and they will probably enter without knocking. They come because they are curious and want to see how the newcomer lives. They come also because they are friendly folk who want the volunteer to feel at home in their midst. And as tokens of their friendliness they bring gifts—a bit of fruit, a pot of soup, freshly popped corn, perhaps a piece of needlework. The constant procession of callers leaves the volunteer little privacy, but it may bring him a host of friends.

The idea that volunteers suffer hardships is widely held. This idea is part of the so-called "Peace Corps image," which presents a picture of a hard-working young person, living in primitive housing, suffering discomfort, but nobly sacrificing himself in a distant land. This "image" had its beginning in the Peace Corps policy of featuring the hardships of Peace Corps life in recruitment so no candidate would misjudge the conditions under which he would serve. The "image" was furthered by articles in the press which emphasized the heroic accomplishments of volunteers in the face of difficulties.

This popular "image" is heartily disliked by many volunteers. It embarrasses them. If they are not experiencing hardships they feel a little guilty. And even if volunteers are meeting physical difficulties, or working very hard, or both, they do not usually like to be labeled as heroes. To be regarded as heroes violates the values that they cherish. A secondary teacher's advice sums up the volunteer's loathing for the sentimental "image." The young man's parting words to me were, "Don't make us saints!"

Volunteers have no special privileges. They are expected to obey the laws and respect the customs of the countries in which they serve. Actually volunteers face certain hazards peculiar to life in underdeveloped countries, one of which is the danger to health.

Lack of sanitation prevails in many underdeveloped countries. Sewage systems are not sufficient. Water supplies are contaminated. Some people lack the habit of using sanitary facilities. Food is not protected. Flies, mosquitoes, and other insects abound. Under these circumstances it is only natural that diseases spread by lack of sanitary precautions are present, sometimes in epidemic proportions.

The Peace Corps is deeply concerned with protecting the health of its volunteers. Each applicant must pass a thorough physical examination to be eligible for the Corps. His health is checked as need arises during his service and he is given another examination when his tour of duty ends. If he suffers illness or accident while serving in the Corps he receives immediate treatment and care. Volunteers are immunized against all likely diseases before they go overseas. The shots are continued when necessary during service abroad. The Peace Corps training program includes instruction in health practices and first aid.

Responsibility for professional health care rests upon the Public Health Service, an agency of the United States Government. Peace Corps physicians detailed to duty by the Public Health Service serve in the host countries. Responsibility for personal health care rests with each Peace Corps volunteer who must safeguard his own health by observing reasonable precautions.

The Peace Corps tour of duty is two years. A volunteer with a satisfactory record may be permitted to extend his service, but extension is not encouraged as a general practice. A volunteer receives a short leave after completing training. While overseas each volunteer is given one month's leave each year and is encouraged to use it for travel in the country where he serves or in nearby countries. Except for an emergency, a volunteer may not return to the United States while serving his tour of duty. He may resign at any time and he may be dropped from the Corps for unsatisfactory service or behavior.

A Peace Corps volunteer is assigned to a location and to a general type of work soon after he arrives in the host country. Both assignments may be changed and sometimes are, if circumstances make such change wise. A volunteer may request a change or a staff member may suggest it, but usually there is mutual agreement on the wisdom of the move before it is actually made.

While a volunteer is on an assignment he is expected to give it his best efforts, which usually means long hours at hard labor. Staff members are willing to help him, but no staff member intends to act as an ever-present boss. A volunteer has been selected in part because he is thought to have initiative, ingenuity, imagination, and creativity. He is supposed to use these qualities to find openings for developing his plans.

A basic policy of the Peace Corps is that each volunteer must, if possible, upgrade the skills and increase the knowledge of his co-workers who are natives of the host country. It is not always possible to carry out this policy. A volunteer may not in every instance have a co-worker, or counterpart. In some cases the counterpart does not want to change his methods nor does he believe that the American volunteer has a better method. It may happen that both volunteer and counterpart are so busy doing the job that there is no time or opportunity for the volunteer to teach or the counterpart to learn new skills.

Yet in spite of difficulties in putting the policy into practice, the worth of the Peace Corps program rests upon this person-to-person process by which skills are transmitted so that projects can be continued. Tom Torres, former volunteer in Colombia, now an Associate Representative in Ecuador, summed it up when he said, "The volunteer should bear in mind that what happens after he leaves is the final measure of his success."

Loss or Gain

A young man from America, visiting in New Delhi, India, went around to the Peace Corps Hostel. This informal lodging is maintained by the Peace Corps Office in India as a stopping place for volunteers who are in the city for a short time. On almost any day a few volunteers drop into the hostel. The young American found several people there when he paid his call.

Curiosity had brought the visitor to the hostel. He wanted to ask the volunteers why they had enlisted in what he considered a foolish undertaking. His questions exploded like corn in a popper. "Why did you join the Peace Corps? What are you doing? Aren't you meeting a lot of problems? What do you expect to get out of all your hard work over here? How can you afford to give two years of your life to this business? What do you expect to do when you go home?"

The volunteers answered the questions, each in his own way. They defended their decision to work with the Peace Corps. Some of them argued with the young man. But the visitor remained unconvinced.

"You know," he said, "you're a bunch of nuts. You work for nothing. You put up with hardships over here. You lose two years when you could be getting ahead. And when you go home you have no job. I tell you, you're nuts!"

The young American's criticism raises a question that needs to be answered. Are those Americans who give two years of their lives to aid underdeveloped countries wasting time and effort?

Perhaps the best answer to the question is to be found in the responses that volunteers gave to four related questions put to them. These questions were:

Why did you join the Peace Corps?

What frustrations have you met?

What rewards have you found?

What do you expect to do when you go home?

Volunteers do not talk freely or frequently about their reasons for joining the Peace Corps. Yet they do sometimes reveal the strong feelings that led them to enlist in this adventure in helping people to help themselves.

The most widely held motive is probably a desire to be useful and helpful, often combined with a very real compassion for the world's less fortunate people. One young woman in Ecuador expressed her sense of obligation in an off-hand way, saying, "Well, a person ought to do something worth-while once in a lifetime."

It was a nurse in Tunisia who implied that a sense of guilt over her own fortunate situation was an added spur. After mentioning her desire to use her nursing skill "to help people," she added, "Maybe I had a little guilty conscience because I was having a life so much better than others."

Compassion for the needy is often mentioned, but seldom with greater feeling than in the words of a young giant in Tunisia. Explaining the motive that drove him to join the Corps, this volunteer said, "I have always had a soft spot in my heart for poor people who lack education."

The sense of compassion is present to some degree in every successful volunteer. Perhaps many volunteers could echo the thought of one young man, nearing the end of a tour of duty in Ecuador, who said, "This experience has changed my life. Now I wonder if I can ever live at home as I did before, knowing of the horrible human need in other lands."

The desire to give other people a better image of the United States is the feeling that impels some volunteers. Most of them regard Peace Corps service as patriotic, though, as one young person put it, "To say I am trying to do something for my country sounds 'corny.'"

Certain of the younger volunteers speak of the influence exerted by President Kennedy as a factor in their decision to join the Peace Corps. One who expressed this thinking said, "President Kennedy made us feel that it was the young people's turn to do something about the mess in the world."

A long interest in international affairs leads naturally to a decision to enlist as a Peace Corps volunteer. So does a taste for working with people more than with things.

A healthy self-interest influences the decision of many volunteers, who see Peace Corps service as an opportunity to become well acquainted with the culture of another land. The

Trainees in Hawaii cut reeds for the roof of a Borneo-type house like those in Sabah and Sarawak, states of federated Malaysia.

desire to travel abroad is another motive often mentioned. A young woman in India put the matter neatly when she said, "I had wanted for a long time to get to another country without joining the army."

A teacher in India related his experience while in college of hearing a world problem discussed by two foreign students with opposite views. He said, "After that I decided to see some of the world for myself and try to understand world problems."

Love of adventure lures volunteers into the Peace Corps. And none who mentioned this motive has been disappointed, for each has found his service to be his greatest adventure.

The Peace Corps provides a period in which young people dissatisfied with their jobs or uncertain of the course they wish their lives to take can find a sense of direction and a test of their own powers. One of these, a teacher in India, said, "I was not sure what I wanted to do. Now I know I want to teach math."

Volunteers see the Peace Corps as a way both to give and to get. In selecting recruits Peace Corps officials look for evidence that the candidate has, to some degree, both motives. Experience has shown that such a volunteer is more likely to stick to his job when the going is rough.

Peace Corps volunteers have frustrations, dozens of them. Far from being an army of uncomplaining saints, they are a corps of typical Americans who tackle their jobs with vigor and voice their complaints in normal fashion.

Americans at home expect complaints from volunteers about physical conditions, but neither returned volunteers nor those still in the field consider physical conditions as a major frustration. The responses of returned volunteers show that only 1 per cent found physical hardship a serious problem.

The deeply ingrained cultural attitude of the local people is probably the greatest frustration to the volunteers. Many countries in which the Peace Corps is working have endured centuries of colonialism. There is usually widespread illiteracy, poverty, malnutrition, and disease. Political leaders have time and again made promises that they did not keep. In the light of these conditions it is small wonder that the natives often greet the enthusiastic suggestions of new volunteers with cold stares or amused glances. They have heard talk like that from self-serving politicians, but they know that nothing came of the glowing prospects. They do not believe that the volunteers' rosy dream will bring them any benefits either.

This apathy and indifference discourages volunteers, but those who succeed learn that they must listen more to the people and talk less. They become friends with the people, win their confidence and trust, perhaps even persuade the people to trust each other. After months of such effort a volunteer is often rewarded by a glimmer of interest upon the part of a few people in improving some specific situation in the community.

Undue respect for tradition often enslaves people in under-developed countries and frustrates Peace Corps volunteers. A volunteer working with a co-operative in Ecuador saw his greatest difficulty as changing the mental attitudes of the men. That he was succeeding was indicated by the comments of an American, not in the Peace Corps, who had observed the project. This observer said in praise of it, "The men have gained self-confidence, developed a sense of responsibility, and learned to trust each other. In fact, they have gained a whole new outlook."

Almost as widespread are the frustrations which arise when a volunteer is thwarted by the regulations of the government in the host country, or handicapped by the poor organization of a government agency. Complaints of "too much bureaucracy," "endless red tape," "unnecessary records" and "no organization" are made by numerous volunteers.

More than half of the volunteers in the Peace Corps are teachers. Many of them express complaints about the demands of the school systems in the countries where they teach. The chief complaint is against the great emphasis upon rote learning and memorization, widely practiced in many countries where volunteers work. In systems in which students are required to pass so-called "external examinations" they prepare for the examination by memorizing facts. The examination questions are made and the answers graded outside the school system, hence the term "external examination." There is an outline, or syllabus, for each course upon which the questions are based. A teacher is expected to follow the syllabus closely. The students insist upon copying into notebooks every fact presented to the class in order that they may memorize it.

American teachers, accustomed to using discussion and problem solving as processes of learning, believe that the extreme emphasis upon memorization is unfortunate. There are signs that the system may in time be modified. In Malaysia the first steps in that direction have been taken. The healthy criticism of Peace Corps volunteers may help produce a better plan. At the same time the experience in a system which places so high a premium upon learning facts may send volunteers back to America in a mood to improve teaching procedures at home. One volunteer teacher observed, "In Malaysia the students have enormous mastery of facts but they do not know how to think; in America our students have learned the process of thinking but they often lack facts. Each system needs to learn something from the other."

Nurses serving as volunteers in some countries have found themselves in conflict with the prevailing standards and practices of medicine. They are also troubled by the discovery that nursing does not enjoy the status that it does in America. Because the Peace Corps holds as a basic policy that each volunteer shall upgrade the skills of his counterpart, it expects its nurses to improve the skills of nurses in the host countries. But many nurses in host countries feel no need for instruction from the Peace Corps nurses. This lack of understanding creates unfortunate human relations.

Some volunteers complain because they are not given enough to do; some because they can see no tangible results of their work; others because they do not consider their work to be significant. A few, perhaps suffering from "the Peace Corps image," complain that their jobs do not offer enough difficulties. A volunteer in Malaysia who enjoyed her work and her living quarters stated this complaint when she said, "I am having the time of my life, but I feel guilty about having such a good time. I should have a job that requires more sacrifice."

Lack of language facility is a very real problem. All volunteers receive language training, but in a country such as India which has many local languages it is not always possible for a volunteer to have all the mastery of languages that he needs. The Peace Corps has increased the amount of language training in an effort to overcome this problem.

The emphasis in host countries upon status irks volunteers. In Ecuador, volunteers who moved into a grass hut were reproved by their counterpart, a social worker, who considered the dwelling too lowly for their status. In India, a teacher, who, with the help of his students, started to move a table, was stopped by the headmaster, who said, "Let me call the servants to move the table."

A sense of status often limits sharply what a worker can do. A volunteer, nursing in Malaysia, said, "Democracy has not penetrated social relationships in this country. A staff nurse cannot even bathe a patient."

Peace Corps volunteers provide daily examples of democracy in action, which is the Corps's answer to the concern with status. The teacher in Sierra Leone who carried his own bags; the nurse in Malaysia who visited with her poorest neighbors; the two women in Ecuador who walked the dusty roads with a delegation of Indians to help them secure water rights; the farm workers in Tunisia who made friends with Bedouins; the young men in India who offered the hospitality of their house to a

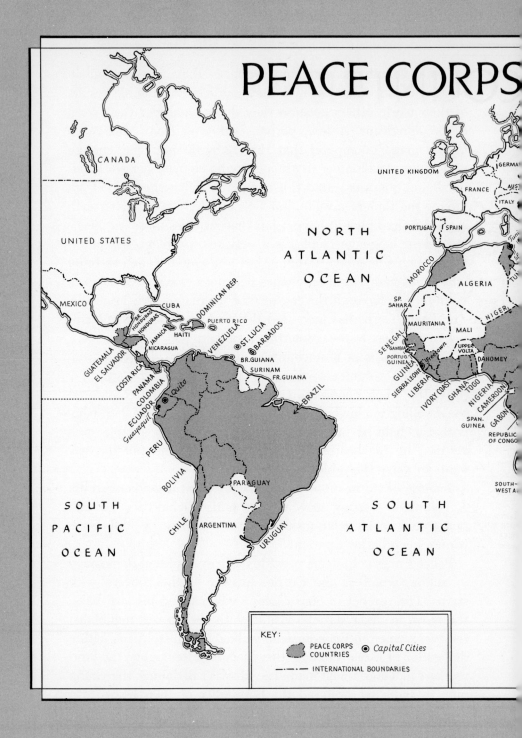

COUNTRIES

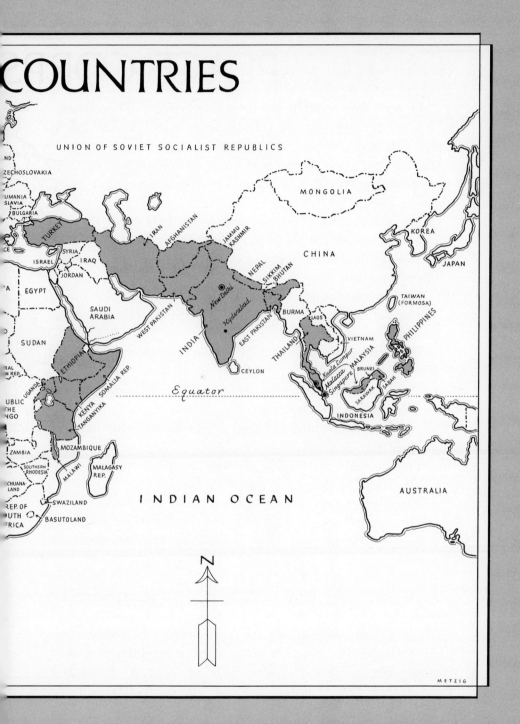

UNION OF SOVIET SOCIALIST REPUBLICS

ZECHOSLOVAKIA
ND
UMANIA
SLAVIA
BULGARIA
CE
TURKEY
SYRIA
ISRAEL
IRAQ
JORDAN
A
EGYPT
SUDAN
SAUDI
ARABIA
IRAN
AFGHANISTAN
WEST PAKISTAN
JAMMU
KASHMIR
NEPAL
SIKKIM
BHUTAN
New Delhi
Hyderabad
INDIA
EAST PAKISTAN
CEYLON
MONGOLIA
CHINA
KOREA
JAPAN
TAIWAN
(FORMOSA)
BURMA
LAOS
THAILAND
VIETNAM
PHILIPPINES
ETHIOPIA
UGANDA
SOMÁLIA REP.
UBLIC
THE
NGO
KENYA
TANGANYIKA
Equator
Kuala Lumpur
Malacca
Singapore
MALAYSIA
BRUNEI
SABAH
SARAWAK
INDONESIA
ZAMBIA
MOZAMBIQUE
SOUTHERN
RHODESIA
MALAWI
MALAGASY
REP.
CHUANA-
LAND
SWAZILAND
REP. OF
UTH
RICA
BASUTOLAND

INDIAN OCEAN

AUSTRALIA

N

METZIG

chauffeur who had no place to stay—these Americans were teaching their country's most important lesson.

"My work has brought me deep satisfaction." These words of a nurse in Malaysia are echoed again and again by Peace Corps volunteers. In spite of frustrations, and sometimes hardships, the volunteers, almost without exception, pronounce their experience rewarding.

And what are the rewards?

The satisfaction of having attempted, in a small way, to remedy some of the ills of the world.

The satisfaction, for some, of having produced tangible improvements.

The satisfaction of personal growth.

The satisfaction, for some, of experience that provided professional growth.

The satisfaction, for many, of having upgraded the skills of workers abroad.

The satisfaction, for some, of having found a new purpose and direction for their lives.

The increased understanding gained by knowing another culture.

The pleasure provided by foreign travel.

The joy of having made new friends.

The appreciation of home gained by being away.

The opportunity to interpret America to other people.

The opportunity to help Americans understand other people.

What will Peace Corps volunteers do when they return home?

Many volunteers continue their education when they complete their service, some in areas of previous interest, but a considerable number in new fields of interest discovered through their Peace Corps experience. Volunteers have already learned that successful Peace Corps service is an asset in receiving the precious graduate scholarships that for many are essential to continued study.

Positions on the Peace Corps staff or in other government agencies and public services will claim some volunteers. There are volunteers still in the field who already have their hopes pointed toward specific types of public service; for example, overseas teaching, work in the foreign aid program, work in the Job Corps and other phases of the poverty program.

Returned volunteers want jobs working with people. A great many volunteers who had never taught before entering service have expressed the intention to teach. Others want to go into other people-to-people endeavors, such as social work or extension service. Some can be expected to engage in work intended to improve racial and economic tensions in America. In the Peace Corps, volunteers have accepted each individual on his own merits and they will not patiently accept less than this attitude when they return home.

Business attracts some volunteers. Their experience will make them especially useful to concerns with overseas operations. Many volunteers want to return to the countries in which they saw service and will welcome a chance to be employed there. However, the Peace Corps experience most prized by volunteers is that which offers them the opportunity to be creative and to act on their own initiative. Volunteers who have had this type of experience seek positions that offer similar freedom of action.

Peace Corps volunteers invest two years of their lives in helping other people help themselves. Does this investment represent for them loss or gain?

Partners in Progress

Eduardo Sotomayor took my husband and me to visit a farm, near Quito, known as the Reproduction Center. The first animals that we saw were a frisky calf and its anxious mother. Mr. Sotomayor said, "That is the first Jersey calf ever born in Ecuador. The calf's mother was shipped from a farm in Vermont."

The cow moved forward, her head lowered, ready to protect her offspring. I retreated toward the barn.

An Indian boy standing nearby walked toward the cow and spoke to her in quiet tones. Mr. Sotomayor, smiling at my alarm, said, "There is no danger. The cow knows Luis and he will keep an eye on her."

"Two eyes might be better," I thought, as I made a cautious move toward the animals. Then I asked, "How did a cow from so far away happen to be sent to Ecuador?"

"She came in a shipment arranged by Heifer Project, Inc. A service club and a church in a Vermont town paid for this cow and the others in the shipment. The foreign aid program of the United States paid the shipping cost. The minister of the Vermont church and another man in the town came to see that the animals arrived safely here at the Reproduction Center."

"Why were the cows brought here?" my husband asked.

"To stay during the quarantine period that is required by law," Mr. Sotomayor replied. Continuing to explain the operation of the plan, he added, "All animals brought through Heifer Project are received and cared for here until the end of their quarantine period."

The man turned to the Indian boy and spoke in Spanish

when he said, "Luis is one of our best caretakers at the Center."

Luis Changoluiza's face glowed at these words of praise. Herding the animals toward the barn, the boy gave a happy little skip that sent the calf into a frolic.

Heifer Project, Inc., is an international agency working in Ecuador and a number of other countries. The particular service that Heifer Project, Inc., renders is the distribution of farm animals to persons who need them and are prepared to care for them. The organization was formed in 1944 and four years later Ecuador received its first shipment of livestock. The first animals distributed there were cattle, but the program rapidly expanded to include sheep, goats, hogs, rabbits, chickens, ducks, geese, turkeys, and bees. Heifer Project also gives assistance in improving crops and in sharing educational information concerning agriculture.

The person who receives an animal promises to give the first-born offspring to someone else in need. Thus the principle of sharing is kept alive by a never-ending chain of gifts.

One of the basic policies established for the Peace Corps stated that volunteers overseas would work for the host government or for private agencies and organizations within the foreign country. In some situations the Peace Corps and the co-operating agency sign a contract. When this is done the agency sends an expert with technical training to supervise the program on which the agency is co-operating.

Heifer Project, Inc., is one of the voluntary agencies with which the Peace Corps co-operates. In Ecuador, as well as in certain other countries, the Peace Corps has a contract with Heifer Project, Inc. Eduardo Sotomayor is the Assistant Coordinator of the Heifer Project—Peace Corps work in Ecuador.

Peace Corps volunteers serving under this contract arrangement in Ecuador work with boys, like Luis Changoluiza, and

A group of boys in Ecuador learn how to start a tree nursery.

sometimes with girls, in agricultural clubs patterned after 4-H clubs in the United States. They also work with adult farmers. The volunteers teach the care and management of the animals provided by Heifer Project. They conduct experimental work to show how crop production can be improved. Their concern is to upgrade farming skills and improve the production of Ecuadorian farms.

CARE is another voluntary group with which the Peace Corps is involved. In Sierra Leone the Peace Corps has a contract with CARE for the administration of the Rural Development Program. It is carried on under the guidance of the CARE Administrator in Sierra Leone. Working under his direction, Peace Corps volunteers have helped the people of the rural villages construct roads, bridges, schoolhouses, dispensaries, water systems, and other public improvements.

The Peace Corps has secured the co-operation of professional and trade associations. An example of co-operation with a professional group is found in Tunisia, where the Peace Corps has a contract with the American Institute of Architects. The Institute provides a highly trained architect, known as the Contractor's Overseas Representative. This man directs the work of a large group of Peace Corps volunteer architects who are moving Tunisia's building program forward rapidly.

A trade association with which the Peace Corps has a contract in Ecuador is the Credit Union National Association, more commonly called CUNA. This world-wide organization helped to establish the Federation of Credit Unions in Ecuador. CUNA has a Contract Overseas Representative in Ecuador who works with the Federation and directs the activities of the Peace Corps volunteers assigned to credit union work.

These volunteers and the field men sent out by the Federation work together in helping to establish and supervise local credit unions. In each local credit union a group of people who have a common bond of interest, e.g., the same occupation or place of residence, combine together to place their savings in the credit union with the privilege of borrowing from it. Since it is difficult in Ecuador for persons of limited means to secure loans the credit union meets a need. At the same time the credit union encourages people to save their money.

Farm organizations assist the Peace Corps program. An example of such co-operation is the contract in Malaysia between the 4-H Club Foundation and the Peace Corps. The Foundation provides an expert in 4-H club work who assists the program carried on by volunteers in organizing and conducting 4-H clubs.

The Peace Corps has the help of a number of colleges and universities in guiding its overseas programs. In Ecuador the Peace Corps has entered into a contract with Springfield College in Massachusetts. The college provides sports and recreational specialists for Ecuador.

Peace Corps volunteers work in some countries under the supervision of the Food and Agricultural Organization, an agency of the United Nations. In Tunisia FAO has operated two experimental farms, with the assistance of a number of volunteers.

Ecuador offers an example of a country in which there is a wide range of co-operative effort. In addition to having contracts with certain organizations, the Peace Corps in Ecuador has less formal arrangements with a number of other groups.

A large program of school construction is going forward in Ecuador. The construction is financed from three sources: the local community in which the school is built, the Ecuadorian government, and the foreign aid program of the United States. This latter program is administered through the Agency for International Development (AID) of the State Department. In Ecuador the Office of School Construction in Quito heads the work. In some instances the Peace Corps has made volunteers available to assist communities in discharging their obligations in school construction.

The Hope Ship is a co-operative effort of physicians to take medical and hospital services to areas of the world where these are lacking. American doctors volunteer their services on the ship for limited periods. The ship puts into a port and serves the health needs of the area in various ways.

In 1964 the Hope Ship was anchored at Guayaquil, Ecuador. One form of service that it rendered was the operation of a nutrition program for infants. The program was especially concerned with teaching mothers how to use food, available even to poor people, to give babies a balanced and nutritious diet. Peace Corps volunteers helped in the nutrition program.

Many people in Ecuador cannot read and write. The Ministry of Education of the Ecuadorian government is seeking to have these people taught as quickly as possible. One organization through which the Ministry works is the Laubach Literacy Foundation, which has developed a fairly easy way, known as the Laubach Method, for teaching reading. In Ecuador, Peace Corps volunteers may take training in using this method. After finishing the training many volunteers teach literacy classes.

A few years ago a regional development organization was set up by the Ecuadorian government to improve economic and living conditions in three southern provinces. This organization is called *Centro de Reconversión Económica,* and commonly known as the Centro. The Peace Corps co-operates with the Centro, making volunteers available to help in its development projects.

The Roman Catholic Church in the United States has sent a group of workers, known as Papal Volunteers, to Ecuador. In one of the cities the Papal Volunteers and a Peace Corps volunteer are working together in an effort to help a local carpenters' co-operative grow strong enough to establish a woodworking factory.

Most host countries offer some form of assistance to the Peace Corps programs within their borders. The amount and type of help varies from country to country. Among the kinds of help a host country might provide are housing, office space, clerical help, in-country transportation, medical care, and assistance on the volunteer's living allowance.

Material support for the Peace Corps program has flowed in from many sources beyond the agencies with which the Peace Corps has established co-operative relationships. Individuals, clubs, school groups, foundations, business firms, and many other organizations have donated money, books, medical supplies, tools, jeeps, and other types of equipment to further the success of Peace Corps projects.

The power of the idea that is the basis of the Peace Corps has reached far beyond the United States. The American Peace Corps had barely celebrated its first birthday when an international conference, organized by the Peace Corps, was held in Puerto Rico. Forty-one countries had representatives with the power to vote at this conference. They voted unanimously to establish a group of officials "to assist in the creation of volunteer assistance programs to developing countries, and where possible to aid these countries in mobilizing their own domestic volunteer groups."

A number of countries have responded to the call and set up national service corps. The length and conditions of service for the volunteers vary from country to country. However, the basic purpose of these service corps of other lands, like that of the Peace Corps, is to help people help themselves.

The international officials authorized in the Puerto Rico meeting also helped to establish the first domestic peace corps. This was organized in El Salvador, a country in Central America. The first El Salvadorean volunteers, after training, were assigned to work with a group of United States Peace Corps volunteers in community development work. Thus El Salvadoreans and Americans became partners in seeking to improve health, education, agriculture, and other aspects of community development.

Other countries laid plans for creating their own volunteer organizations to carry on development work within their own borders. In the United States, President Lyndon B. Johnson, declaring a war on poverty, appointed Sargent Shriver to head the agency authorized by Congress to put the program into action. The program had several aspects, one of which was the creation of a domestic service corps, Volunteers in Service to America, known as VISTA.

The first concern of the Peace Corps is to render service to the people of underdeveloped countries. The volunteer is the agent for promoting self-help projects by means of which the people may, step-by-step, overcome their difficulties. In those situations in which helping people to help themselves can be better done through co-operative effort, the Peace Corps works with other agencies. Such agencies and the Peace Corps thus become partners in progress.

2. AT WORK IN ECUADOR

Boys with a Future

"A shine, Señor? Have a shine?"

A small, bright-eyed boy addressed his question to a man hurrying across a plaza in downtown Quito. Without a word the man stepped around the boy and moved on. With a shrug of his narrow shoulders, the shoeshine boy darted toward a second man crossing the plaza. Once more he called, "A shine, Señor?" This time luck was with him. The man paused, then dropped upon a bench beside the walk and thrust out his foot.

Manuel Moquinche lifted a tiny stool from his shoeshine box, seated himself in front of the man, and fell to work. He spread polish with expert fingers and cracked his long polishing rag as he shined the shoe glistening bright. The man glanced down at the boy. His idle gaze took in the blue cap perched jauntily on a mop of black hair and the blue jacket, but his interest quickened when he noticed a white patch on the boy's sleeve. On the patch were the letters C.M.T.

Pointing to the patch, the man asked, "What do the letters mean?"

"They stand for Centro del Muchacho Trabajador," Manuel replied. With a final crack of the polishing rag the nimble brown fingers finished their task. The boy looked up at his customer, and added, "I belong to the Centro. That's why I can wear this blue jacket and cap."

"I suppose you are proud to wear your Centro's uniform," the man remarked.

"Of course," the boy replied. "And because I have earned the right to wear it the police allow me to work here in the Plaza de la Independencia."

The man fished sixty centavos from his pocket and handed them to the boy. Then, glancing around the plaza where other blue-clad boys were plying their trade, the man said, "Since belonging to the Centro gives you the privilege of working in the city's most important plaza, I suppose becoming a Centro member is the end you all seek."

Manuel was silent for a moment as he gathered the tools of his trade into his shoeshine box. Then an impish grin lighted his face as he said, "You've got it turned the wrong way round, Señor. Like Bernie says, 'Belonging to Centro is not the end for us boys, it's just the beginning.'"

Manuel Moquinche was one of sixty boys in Quito, Ecuador, who found the beginning of a new way of life through the Centro del Muchacho Trabajador, or the Working Boy's Center. And his friend Bernie was one of the Peace Corps volunteers whose work made the boy's club a success.

There are about a thousand shoeshine boys in Quito, as well as numerous other boys who sell cigarettes, candy, chewing gum, newspapers and lottery tickets on the streets. The boys often begin their lives as street workers by the time they are six or seven years old. All are poor. Many are orphans, but those who have families are usually helping to support them with their earnings from small sales or sixty-centavo shoeshines.

In Quito the shoeshine boys created a special problem because they all wanted to work in the Plaza de la Independencia. This square in the heart of the city, always well-filled with people, offered the largest concentration of possible customers. Keen competition combined with a spirit of every-boy-for-himself led to fights. When the police grew tired of restoring peace among the squabbling shoeshine boys they ordered all of the boys permanently out of the Plaza de la Independencia.

A British foreign service officer, Robert Copping, stationed in Quito, heard of the boys' plight. He found some other interested people and with their help organized the Centro.

These sponsors secured funds from donations and benefits and rented two small rooms to serve as a clubhouse. When the police were assured that the Centro would regulate the boys' work they granted permission for a limited number of shoeshine boys to work each day in the Plaza de la Independencia. But who was to have the privilege of working in the plaza? And how was the Centro to be regulated?

When the sponsors tried to find answers to these questions they realized their need for a man to give close attention and direction to the Centro's program. They sought help from the Peace Corps and for a time Samuel McPhetres worked on the project. When Samuel's Peace Corps service ended another volunteer, Bernard Stock, took over the responsibility for directing the program.

The Centro uniform became the regulating agency. Working areas were designated by different color jackets and caps. Only boys in blue could work in the Plaza de la Independencia, but in order that all boys could have a turn at this most desirable location, jackets were given out each Monday morning on a rotating basis. A boy wore the coveted blue and shined shoes in the plaza one week, then took his turn in other locations. Discipline in the Centro was maintained by withholding the uniforms if the rule about rotation was violated. A boy without the Centro's jacket with the magic arm patch was at a disadvantage. But two chances were given each boy who had had his jacket withheld, to earn again the privilege of wearing the Centro's badge of honor.

With the help of the sponsors, a shower and toilet were installed at the clubrooms. Both were unknown luxuries to the boys, but under Bernie Stock's guidance they soon mastered the use of the new equipment. A barber came at intervals to the clubrooms to cut hair. With hot baths, haircuts, and clean jackets, Centro boys became a sharp-looking crew.

In Quito each working boy is required to have a work permit, but many had never secured their papers. When the police began to enforce the law on work permits the Centro helped the boys get the necessary documents. In order to hold a permit a boy must attend one of the three daily sessions of school, but many boys had gone to school little or not at all. Under Bernie Stock's leadership the Centro boys were enrolled in school. In addition, classes for older boys were set up at enlarged club-rooms in order that these boys might catch up on neglected studies. The classes were held from three to three-thirty each day, a time when rain often falls in Quito and drives shoeshine boys and street merchants indoors. A teacher provided by the Ministry of Education taught arithmetic, grammar, and geography. Bernie Stock taught two boys who were totally illiterate to read. One was Manuel Moquinche, who, after a few months of instruction by the Laubach Method, was reading books with joy and understanding.

Quito shoeshine boys talk to Sam McPhetres about forming a club.

When lessons ended rolls and milk provided by CARE were well received. A game or a movie shown by courtesy of one of the embassies in Quito furnished a happy climax for a work-filled day.

Always Bernie Stock kept before his boys the idea that being a member of the Centro was only the beginning of a better life than was possible for a shoeshine boy or a street merchant. One of his concerns was to help the boys learn new skills and find better jobs. As he saw boys secure work in households, bakeries, candy factories, and shoe shops this Peace Corps volunteer knew that the Centro was opening new doors of opportunity for some of Quito's working boys.

When we flew into Quito, the capital of Ecuador, we were greeted cordially by Mr. Erich Hofmann, the Deputy Director, who in the absence of the Director was the head of the Ecuador Peace Corps program. Mr. Hofmann contacted the Associate Representatives in charge of the Regional offices and with their co-operation set up a schedule that enabled us to travel over the country and interview almost fifty volunteers.

We flew from Quito to some of the cities. To reach small towns and remote villages we rode with the Associate Representatives as they made their rounds among the volunteers. This travel was entirely by Peace Corps jeeps and was often over rough and dusty roads.

As we traveled over Ecuador we became sharply aware of the great differences in surface, climate, and cultural conditions that exist in the country. These differences have caused Ecuador to be called "Country of Contrasts."

Country of Contrasts

In the early sixteenth century the land now called Ecuador was part of an Indian empire ruled by an emperor known as the Inca. When the Spaniard Francisco Pizarro invaded the empire he put the Inca to death and established Spanish rule over the area.

The land was a Spanish colony for some three hundred years. But in time the spirit of revolt stirred in Ecuador. The battle that won Ecuador's freedom from Spain was fought on May 24, 1822. For a few years Ecuador was in a union with two other countries, but in 1830 it withdrew from the union and declared itself an independent nation.

The central government is administered from Quito, the capital. Ecuador is divided into eighteen provinces, each of which has a provincial capital and a governor appointed by the central government.

The key to the location of Ecuador is its name, which means "equator." The equatorial line crosses the country, which is bordered by Peru on the south and east and Colombia on the north. On the west Ecuador is bordered by the Pacific Ocean.

Ecuador has three natural regions. Two ranges of the Andes Mountains run nearly north and south from one end of the country to the other. Between the two Andean ranges lies an elevated plateau divided by cross ranges into a number of valleys. This mountainous backbone of Ecuador is called the Sierra. In sharp contrast to the Sierra is the region which reaches from the foot of the western range of the Andes to the Pacific Coast. For the most part this region is a flat plain cut by rivers that carry water from the Andes. East of the Andes is a region, covering about half the area of Ecuador, known as the Oriente. It is an area of jungle-covered land stretching from the Andes to the eastern boundary of the country.

Because Ecuador sits directly upon the equator, a traveler might expect to find constantly hot temperatures throughout the country, but such is not the case. The high elevation of the Sierra causes the temperatures to be pleasantly cool in the mountain valleys and cold on the high plateaus and peaks.

Most of the coastal plain is saved from extreme heat by breezes blowing from a cold ocean current which flows in the Pacific near the Ecuadorian coast. There are two seasons in this region. The hot, rainy season extends from late December to May, and the cooler dry season covers the remainder of the year. There is, however, a hot, dry strip near the border with Peru.

The Oriente has a tropical climate. With abundant rainfall and high temperatures this is a region of lush plant growth.

About 40 per cent of the people of Ecuador are pure Indian, while another 40 per cent are mixed Indian-white. The latter are known as *mestizos* or *cholos*. The remainder of the Ecuadorians are whites or Negroes. There has been no recent census covering the whole nation, but it is thought that Ecuador has approximately four and a half million people.

The official language in Ecuador is Spanish, but many Indians use tribal tongues. Quechua, the principal language used in the ancient Indian empire, is the most widely used Indian tongue.

Most of Ecuador's people make their living working on the land. The Oriente, still largely a jungle, does not now have much agriculture, but if plans for opening up this region succeed, it may become important for the production of crops such as sugar cane and tropical fruits. Roads are being built into the Oriente and the government is encouraging people to move there.

The coastal plain produces practically all of the country's

agricultural exports. Bananas lead the list. In fact, Ecuador exports more bananas than any other country in the world. Other agricultural products of the coastal region include coffee, rice, sugar cane, and cacao, from which cocoa and chocolate are made.

The Sierra produces most of the food consumed in Ecuador. Because of the elevation, which gives much of this area a temperate climate, potatoes and grains — wheat, corn, barley, and rye — are the leading crops. About half of the land in the Sierra can be cultivated. The remainder is too rugged, too high, or too dry, but more than half the people in the country live in this region.

Until recent years agriculture in the Sierra has been backward. Poor methods of work and the system of land distribution have held down production. Today, many farmers in the Sierra are learning to use fertilizers, to protect their crops from insects and diseases, to use machinery, and to improve their livestock. There still remains a serious problem concerning land distribution, which the nation's leaders, both in and out of the government, are seeking to solve.

The problem goes back to Spanish colonial days. During that period much of the fertile valley land in the Sierra was granted in large tracts to persons whom the Spanish rulers wished to honor or reward. The Indians living on the land were placed under the care of the landowner and were obliged to do such work as the owner required of them. In exchange for this service the landowner was expected to care for the Indians and teach them the Christian religion. This feudal system has been modified in recent years, but the greater part of the best land in the Sierra is still in large estates called *haciendas*, operated by landowners known as *hacendados*.

Under this land system the head of each Indian family was granted the use of a small plot of land near his hut. The Indian was allowed to cultivate this plot, called a *huasipungo*, for his own purposes when he was not working for the large land-owner.

All of the Sierra Indians do not live on haciendas. A few tribes still hold, in common ownership, tribal grants received in colonial days. Still other Indians own individual plots, but these are usually very small and often they are located on steep mountain slopes where cultivation is difficult. Since such small holdings rarely yield enough to support a family, the owners often hire themselves out as workers on haciendas or in nearby towns.

There is little industry in Ecuador, though the manufacture of textiles has some importance and fine woolens are exported. Many of the articles used in everyday living are produced in small workshops or in the homes.

One home industry, the making of "Panama" hats, produced a valuable article for export. These hats, woven largely by women, were made from the fiber of the toquilla palm. The hats became a popular article for sale to tourists in Panama and thus received their name. When this hat became less fashionable, people in Ecuador who had made their living weaving the hats were in distress.

Craftsmen in Ecuador produce excellent wood carvings and gold and silver jewelry of exquisite design. Hand-woven woolen materials combine beauty and utility. Some of the Indian tribes are distinguished for their excellent craft work, one of the best known being the Otavalo tribe, whose members are especially noted for their weaving.

Great poverty exists in Ecuador, yet there is a growing number of people each year who enjoy a rising standard of living. This improvement has followed increases in educational and economic opportunity among the people.

Differences in racial background, education, and wealth have created in Ecuador several distinct cultural groups. Each such group has its own set of values derived from its own cultural pattern. One of the country's needs is greater mutual understanding and co-operation among these different groups.

The majority of the Ecuadorian Indians live in the Sierra. These Indians have not only maintained their own ways of living as distinguished from the whites, but also the differing cultural pattern of the various tribes. The tribal differences are shown in dress, customs, and language. Yet in spite of such differences, Sierra Indians are alike in several ways. They have great love for the land even when they do not own it. They have a strong sense of mutual obligation. A favor received must be returned. They are usually devout Roman Catholics. They respect tradition, resist change, and tend to be suspicious of strangers. They stress tribal loyalty and join willingly in a system of collective work known as the *minga*, in which they work together on large projects that offer common benefits. The minga is of ancient origin. It was used by the Incas and perhaps earlier. It is used today to build schoolhouses, roads, irrigation ditches, and other public works.

Ecuador is a land of social and physical contrasts, a land of differing cultural patterns, a land where there is wealth and poverty, learning and ignorance. It is a land whose people are deeply concerned about status and yet are kindly and courteous. It is a land that for centuries knew little change. Yet today the winds of change are blowing in the high Andean valleys, on the rich coastal plains, and even in the remote Oriente. Ecuadorians are setting their sights on a better life for their people. Many international agencies are working in Ecuador to speed this new day, and not the least of these is the American Peace Corps.

Better Life in the Barrios

One day Jim Samiljan took us to see the *barrio* (a ward or district of a city) in Guayaquil where he worked. Our first visit was to the Mildred Allen Community Center, which could be reached only by a narrow foot path.

We stepped gingerly along the path behind the young Peace Corps volunteer, for we knew that a misstep would plunge us into the mud. Beside the path stood houses built of bamboo. These structures, called *caña* houses in Ecuador, were built on reclaimed land along the estuary. Some of the building lots had been filled, but many houses were elevated on stilts. At high tide water from the estuary swept under the houses on stilts. During storms even those on higher ground were flooded. The tides carried sewage and garbage out to sea, but pools of water were left behind to grow stagnant and muddy flats lay waiting to trap the unsuspecting foot.

In the Mildred Allen Center we found a group of neatly dressed women having a class in needlework. The small caña house was in a buzz of movement and chatter as the women learned to ornament with machine embroidery the dresses they were making. The teacher, a native of the barrio, explained to us that on other days there were classes in plain sewing, cooking, and English.

"About one hundred women use the center now, and when we get a new center we expect to have activities for the men, too," Jim Samiljan explained.

We expressed our wonder that a new center could be achieved in such a poor barrio. Jim told us that the people had formed a committee and were already raising money for the new center. The committee had sponsored benefit dances and

Jim Samiljan leads visitors past cana houses in Huancavilca Barrio.

movies to get funds and had secured an order from a factory that produced mosquito nets to use over beds. Women in the barrio sewed the nets and gave half of their earnings to the community center fund.

The young volunteer led us out of the Mildren Allen Center. Pointing across the acres of mudflats crisscrossed by built-up walks and cane bridges, he said, "When Walter Szczepanek and I came to this barrio to undertake community development work, the people were suspicious of us. They had heard a lot of promises for improvements from politicians seeking votes. They had learned that often, with the election over, nothing came from the promises. But Walter and I made no promises. We had nothing to give them except our help in solving their own problems. So, little by little, the people changed their attitude. They are no longer waiting for someone else to improve conditions here. They have set about doing the job themselves."

Huancavilca Barrio on the outskirts of Guayaquil offers a typical example of community development as it is practiced in Ecuador. The work of community improvement is carried on both in cities and in rural areas. The work in cities and in suburban areas is called urban community development. The work in villages and rural areas is known as rural community development.

Community development seeks to have the people of a community recognize the problems that obstruct their progress and develop plans to overcome these problems, as far as possible, through their own efforts. It is a program to help people learn to help themselves. The need for community development in Ecuador, as in most Latin American countries, is urgent because people are moving in large numbers from rural areas to the cities. This movement creates problems which, if left unsolved, may lead to worse conditions of living as the cities become more crowded.

Credit unions sometimes play an important part in furthering urban community development. There is nothing about the nature of a credit union that makes it useful only in urban areas, but in Ecuador these groups have been organized more rapidly in urban than in rural communities. The credit union movement has grown steadily in Ecuador and has reached its greatest popularity in the coastal region.

Each credit union must be legally authorized through the Federation of Credit Unions in Ecuador. The Federation operates under the Ecuadorian Ministry of Social Welfare, which in turn acts through the Department of Co-operatives. In order to be legally authorized a credit union must meet certain standards and follow certain practices.

Because of the great demand in Ecuador for credit unions, the Peace Corps was invited to provide volunteers who would share the work of organizing and supervising local credit unions with field men from the Federation. The Peace Corps accepted this responsibility and trained volunteers specifically for the work.

Dick Barr was one of the first group of Peace Corps volunteers to receive such training. Dick was stationed at Ibarra but assigned to work with a number of credit unions in that area. His activities were typical. He supervised the operation of the existing credit unions, helped the officers learn how to realize the full usefulness of these organizations, and organized new unions.

Jon Wills' assignment covered eight credit unions in Guayaquil and two in outlying towns. He performed the usual functions of supervision, education, and organization and was pleased at the end of six months to have his unions keeping their books properly. However, Jon saw his function as more than teaching double-entry bookkeeping. He wanted to see the unions in his group become leading forces in community development.

In the town of Vinces, about sixty miles north of Guayaquil, Jon saw his ambition taking shape as a reality. Within six months after a credit union in Vinces was formed, it had joined with another community group to raise money and have built a four-room concrete-block schoolhouse. When the Hope Ship nutrition training class was held in Guayaquil the Vinces credit union sent a woman volunteer to take the course. She returned and found seven other women to help her carry out the program in Vinces. They were soon working with thirty mothers, teaching them how to feed their babies and weighing the infants to check their progress.

Jon Wills praised credit unions because they taught thrift, provided a source for necessary borrowing, and trained people to work together. However, he expressed what he believed to be their greatest usefulness when he said, "A credit union can be a key to community development."

El Cisne Barrio is a stretch of land on the outskirts of Guayaquil. Some of the area is a swamp over which the tides flow;
some is above normal tide level. The principal street is covered
with crushed rock; all other streets are ankle-deep in dust during the dry season and equally deep in mud when the rains
fall. Many of the dwellings are caña houses, some are of bricks,
a few have an outer covering of cement.

Metal oil drums at every intersection serve as water barrels,
one for each family. Into the barrels the water tank on its
weekly round delivers the barrio's only water supply. There in
the uncovered barrels the water stands, until dipped out and
carried to serve household needs.

In every way that the eye can judge this is a dreary barrio.
Its only modern convenience is electricity. Its only tie with the
world is the bus service, by means of which a traveler may
jounce over the rough road leading to the city. But the visitor
who probes beyond appearance discovers that the winds of
progress are blowing in El Cisne. The people know what they
need and they are determined to make their barrio a better
place in which to live.

When Michael Conniff went as a Peace Corps volunteer to
El Cisne he made the people of the barrio his friends. Having
accepted him as a friend, the citizens began to discuss their
needs with him and to listen to his suggestions that they could
meet some of these needs through a credit union. These dis-
cussions led a group of citizens to form a credit union.

When Michael's tour of duty ended Dave Zimmerman followed him as El Cisne's Peace Corps volunteer. In Dave's first
four months in the barrio the credit union doubled in size to
reach 143 members. Recognizing the opportunities that its new
strength offered, the organization became the action group in
the barrio.

Most of the people in El Cisne had employment. Many of
them owned their houses. Others wanted to build, but building
or repairing houses was hindered because of the difficulty in

securing building materials. Dealers in the city did not want to deliver small orders of materials to this distant point.

The credit union solved this problem by organizing a Deposit of Materials for construction. They secured a site beside a neighborhood store where the materials could be deposited. They bought building materials in quantity at wholesale prices and sold them to people in the barrio as cheaply as possible. The storekeeper, a member of the credit union, agreed to care for the needs of customers who came to buy. And come they did! In the first two months of operation the Deposit sold five hundred sacks of cement, as well as other articles, and the sounds of building were heard in the barrio.

A one-room structure used as a community center served as the credit union office. It was also the meeting place for classes in English, sewing, cooking, child care, mechanics, nutrition, reading, and writing. The credit union decided that an addition to the center was needed and straightway launched a campaign to raise funds. They sponsored benefit movies, held dances, and served suppers. As funds for the addition grew, mutual trust increased. The people were learning to work together for a common goal.

There was no way in the barrio to spread news except by word of mouth. The credit union decided to publish a monthly news sheet. The little paper explained the work of the credit union and the advantages of membership, but it also carried news of community development in other barrios, related current happenings and announced future events in El Cisne Barrio. The paper, which began with four pages, was soon carrying six pages in each issue.

Dave Zimmerman found local reporters and taught them to write acceptable copy. He set other citizens to work securing advertising, arranging for printing, and managing distribution. The newspaper can continue without the help of a volunteer to serve as a common bond drawing the people into co-operative action.

Dave and the credit union tackled one problem after another. They secured a water supply and set up a lunch program at the local school and were soon working on plans for further projects. Under their leadership El Cisne Barrio became a better place in which to live.

We spent a morning in a kindergarten, and at the close of the session we overheard a conversation between a small boy and his mother. The boy said, "I do not want to go home. I like it here." Small Ricardo settled himself on a bench and spoke firmly.

"You can come again tomorrow to the kindergarten," his mother replied. "But now it is time to go home."

Ricardo shook his head vigorously. "No, I stay. We had fun here today."

Young Ricardo had indeed had fun, as had fifty other children who that day had attended the newly organized kindergarten at Cerro Santa Ana Center in Guayaquil. The children had listened to a story, seen a film, sung songs, learned the colors, counted, and played games. Their shining faces, as well as Ricardo's words, attested to their happiness in their new experiences.

The kindergarten was held in a crude wooden building, newly built for a community center. The lot on which the building stood was strewn with rubble, but it served as a playground for the kindergarten children. The new building was unpainted. It had no water. Its only furnishings were a few tables and chairs and some backless benches.

Margaret Elberson and Judith O'Neill, nicknamed Kelly, were Peace Corps volunteers assigned to work in the area. Soon after they arrived they began talking to parents about organizing a kindergarten. At first only two or three persons were interested, but from this unpromising beginning a wave of enthusiasm developed and eighty children were enrolled.

The needs of the kindergarten were endless—supplies, water connection, paint on the walls, play equipment, a clean playground, and money for operation. But the kindergarten did have an expert teacher; Señora Gladys Buitrón, a teacher in the afternoon session of a local school, gave her service at the kindergarten each morning. Girls from the two local universities helped, and the School of Social Work offered guidance. Margaret Elberson served as director and Kelly came two mornings a week with her guitar to sing with the children. With many needs unmet, Peace Corps volunteers, with the help of an expert teacher, created a happy learning situation for young children.

"Today we sold this wardrobe," Alan Lambert said, pointing to a big clothes press. "The buyer came into the shop to order one made, expecting to wait two months for it to be finished. He was delighted to get a ready-made one immediately."

The carpenter shop in Ibarra, where a dozen carpenters worked together, offered a service heretofore unknown in this Ecuadorian city. By pooling their services and a small part of their earnings the carpenters were able to make certain articles of furniture and have them ready for sale when customers appeared. Tables, chairs, and wardrobes found ready sale.

Through the centuries carpenters in Ecuador did their work with hand tools, each man in his own small shop. In Ibarra a project to improve the lot of carpenters was launched by the joint efforts of Peace Corps volunteers and a Papal Volunteer. The project soon became an effort to unite carpenters into a larger working unit, which in turn developed into an informal co-operative.

When first opened, the carpenter shop received a loan from a Catholic agency for the purchase of tools and materials. It was provided with temporary quarters in a church-owned building. It had encouragement from a Papal Volunteer. But the

direction and guidance of the project became the work of Alan
Lambert, a Peace Corps volunteer.

Alan found that he had two responsibilities. One was to help
the carpenters make their co-operative venture an economic
success. The other was to help them learn to work together.

The men understood the need to do satisfactory work in order
to increase production and thus to increase their own earnings.
They accepted Alan's suggestions that furthered these ends.
Customers soon came and the shop turned out flooring, doors,
window frames, and furniture.

Alan found that his second responsibility was harder to carry
out than the first. The carpenters had always worked inde-
pendently of each other. They had had no experience in co-
operation. Neither had they had any training in the processes
by which a joint venture must be managed.

The new techniques necessary for working successfully in a
co-operative had to be acquired on a day-to-day basis. Alan
helped the men develop a list of responsibilities in the shop and
a list of committees needed to discharge the responsibilities.
Both lists were posted in the shop. Committees were appointed
on a two-weeks rotating basis, with everyone serving on a committee.

Alan appointed the first officers. He named one man who
protested that he could never do what was expected of him,
but, encouraged by Alan's confidence in him, the man blossomed into self-reliant activity. When the appointed officers
completed their terms, an election was held and the men chose
their own leaders.

Shop meetings gave the men an opportunity to discuss their
problems. They began to plan for future improvements. They
explored the possibility of forming a credit union. They sup-
ported the plan advanced by the Papal Volunteer and Alan to
seek a government loan and establish a woodworking factory
on a co-operative basis to provide employment for more men

and increase the earning power of each carpenter. Under Alan Lambert's guidance, the carpenters learned to improve their own situation.

Volunteers in Ecuador engaged in community development were often involved with several activities all going forward at the same time. Kathleen Vitale was such a volunteer. She taught art one day a week at the School of Fine Arts. She helped conduct a swimming program. She taught an English class and found among her students leaders ready to help with neighborhood programs. She organized cooking classes that were conducted in the neighborhood center and sewing classes in homes.

Antoinette Unis shows Guayaquil women how to make cake frosting.

The work that touched Kathleen's heart most deeply was her service in the Hope Ship nutrition program. "Ecuador is a nation of sick people," Kathleen remarked. In the program to improve infant feeding she saw one way to improve the ill health that plagued many Ecuadorians.

One day when I was in Kathleen's apartment a woman carrying a tiny child came to the door. "Will you weigh my granddaughter?" the woman asked.

Upon receiving Kathleen's consent the grandmother came into the apartment. She placed the year-old child on the scales provided by Hope Ship to nutrition workers and watched anxiously while Kathleen studied the recording bar, which showed that the baby weighed only twelve pounds. The grandmother stated that the baby had been fed little except milk.

Kathleen Vitale explained to the grandmother why the baby must have solid food. With a strainer from her own kitchen Kathleen demonstrated how beans, bananas, and other Ecuadorian foods could be puréed for baby food. The young volunteer gave the woman a Hope Ship leaflet on infant feeding and explained its meaning. When the woman rose to leave, she spoke fervent thanks to Kathleen.

The small shop on one of Cuenca's main streets was crowded with goods. Sweaters, purses, buttons, and scarfs competed for space with embroidered ponchos designed for evening wear. Mats and squares made from the fiber of Ecuador's cabulla plant crowded the showcases. A giant hooked rug hung from a balcony. An artfully designed chair with seat made of leather thongs stood at one side. A guitar lay on a table.

The shop managed by Perry Gates for the Central Materno Infantil was in business. The Central is a welfare organization. The profits from the sale of goods in the shop help support a kindergarten and other good works carried on by the Central. However, the shop provided an outlet for hand-made articles produced by Ecuadorian craftsmen. It was in the interest of providing such a market that two Peace Corps volunteers became involved.

Ignacio Peri, a volunteer with a flair for the arts, designed articles for native workers to produce, while Perry Gates managed the business of production and selling. Some of the articles were made in homes, others in a workshop operated by the Central. The regional development organization, Centro de Reconversión, provided some necessary funds to help establish the shop. This organization's interest was in providing a market for goods produced in the region, where serious unemployment prevails.

The list of the activities of urban community development workers was all but endless. Teaching classes of adults, finding teachers for vocational classes, training and supervising visitors for nutrition programs, establishing libraries, directing recreational programs, guiding co-operatives and credit unions, operating boys' clubs, creating markets, starting lunch programs, doing city planning—these and many other activities of Peace Corps volunteers help to improve life in Ecuadorian cities.

Improving Rural Living

We went exploring in the countryside near San Gabriel, a town in northern Ecuador. Our mission was to see the sheep which had won the prize as the champion ewe of Ecuador. In San Gabriel we picked up the local agent of the Agricultural Extension Service. Under his guidance, we jolted along in a Peace Corps jeep driven by Tom Torres, until we reached the farm home of Victor Guachán.

Victor was the owner of the Corriedale ewe which a few months before our visit had won the championship at the Holstein Friesian Association Fair held in Quito. At the farm we learned that Victor was away from home, but his father led us to the pasture where the prize ewe was grazing. Victor's two little sisters were herding several sheep, for Victor owned not only the ewe, but a Corriedale ram and several other less valuable animals.

Mr. Guachán was pleased to learn that people from faraway North America wanted to hear of his son's success. He sent one of the small girls scurrying to the farmhouse to bring the newspaper containing Victor's picture and the story about his triumph at the fair. He gave us a detailed account of Victor's progress in working in an agricultural club called Los Compesinos, whose members were aided by Larry Sandvol, a Peace Corps volunteer, and Mr. Antonio Jacho, the Chief of the Agricultural Extension Agency in San Gabriel. Mr. Guachán looked on happily while we took a picture of the prize-winning ewe. Then he and the small girls posed for us. A chill wind from the Andes swept across the pasture, causing the girls to wrap their shawls closely about their shoulders, but the smile on Mr. Gaucháns' face was warm and friendly when he said goodby.

Victor Guachán was one of many 4-F Club members whose success created a new spirit in rural Ecuador. The 4-F clubs are modeled after the 4-H Clubs in the United States and they carry on a similar program. The name 4-F derives from four Spanish words: *fe*, meaning faith, *fecundidad*, meaning fruitfulness or fertility, *fortaleza*, meaning force or strength, and *felicidad*, meaning happiness. The club symbol is a four-leaf clover with a letter F on each of the four leaflets and the number 4 in the center of the emblem. The club program grew rapidly after it was introduced in Ecuador. In July 1964 there were eighty-four clubs with twenty-one hundred members in the country. Club members, who may be either boys or girls, range in age from about ten to twenty years. The clubs are under the Ministry of Development of the Ecuadorian government, which provides immediate supervision to the clubs through the Agricultural Extension Service. Peace Corps volunteers have been useful in assisting with 4-F Club projects.

Within a club the members may have many different activities. While sheep-raising has been especially popular, club members also raise other animals and grow gardens and farm crops. They also do spinning, weaving, and sewing and engage in home improvement projects.

The animals raised by 4-F Club members in Ecuador are provided through Heifer Project, Inc. The animals are all purebred and registered. They are flown from the United States, often in a plane fitted for the purpose and dubbed "Noah's Ark." In each case in which animals are given there is careful instruction on their care, and continuing supervision for a time to insure the success of the project.

Adults, as well as 4-F Club members, may receive animals under the Heifer program, if they comply with necessary conditions for animal care. Adults also receive supervision in management of the animals.

Sheep raising in the San Gabriel area, developed from 4-F Club work, brought a new spirit and increased prosperity. San

Animals received through Heifer Project, Inc., contribute to much-improved living conditions for Ecuadorian people near San Gabriel.

Gabriel is in a region of mountains and valleys. It has good pastures because a cool, rainy climate causes grass to grow well. However, the native sheep raised there yield only about four pounds of wool per sheep at a shearing. Purebred sheep introduced through 4-F Clubs usually yield ten to twenty-five pounds each and Victor's ram recently produced a twenty-eight pound fleece. Wool production was also increased by crossing native and purebred sheep. The better yield of wool enabled farm families to have more warm clothing and still have surplus wool to sell.

The same type of improvement that occurred at San Gabriel took place in other areas. The 4-F Clubs have been an important factor in rural development in Ecuador.

Peace Corps volunteers work with adults, as well as with young people, in agricultural improvement. Stanley Wojtasik in Tulcan was such a volunteer. One project in which he participated was in a striking setting high on a hillside above a main highway. A traveler rounding a bend saw experimental plots stretching up the hillside. One plot was planted to grain without fertilization. Other plots, similarly planted, had received various types and amounts of fertilizer. The effect of fertilization was so evident that no traveler could miss the lesson taught by the experimental plots.

John Snead was the first volunteer to serve in San Joaquin *Parroquia* (a township or district in rural Ecuador). The principal business in the parroquia was raising flowers and vegetables to sell. John, who had college training in floriculture, was sent to give the growers technical assistance. He went into the fields, tested soil, checked plants for diseases, and advised on fertilizers and sprays to be used. He demonstrated proper spraying, using a sprayer borrowed from Heifer Project.

John showed the value of using good seed, especially hybrid seed. He rented a plot of land, borrowed a tractor, and planted flowers and vegetables, using the best seeds he could obtain. Successful production on this plot was convincing proof that money spent to secure good seed was well spent.

For twenty years San Joaquin Parroquia had been trying to get a ditch constructed to bring water for irrigation. Soon after John arrived a community committee secured help on such a project from the Centro de Reconversión Económica.

A ditch, between four and five miles in length, carried water from a river to the parroquia. Every Friday a minga was held to provide laborers to dig the ditch. The completion of the ditch called for a community celebration, which was carried out with great gusto. The people gathered at the headgates of the irrigation ditch, where a priest blessed the waters. The crowd then moved to the San Joaquin plaza. There speeches were made and certificates of honor were given to the men who had helped to dig the ditch. A great outdoor feast followed at which the people ate pork boiled in fat over open fires, *mote* (hominy), and *empanadas* (cheese-filled fried cakes).

While this feast was eaten in the plaza distinguished guests were entertained at a banquet provided by the Cuenca Golf Club, which received water from the irrigation project. John Snead was one of the distinguished guests. The banquet menu included chicken noodle soup with mote, roasted *cuy* (guinea pig), vegetables, and champagne.

Richard Wells was a versatile volunteer assigned to community development in Columbe. This town, whose people are largely mestizos, had learned to use committees before Richard arrived, but he soon observed that the same people served on all the committees. The young volunteer set about broadening the base of participation by stimulating a variety of activities and drawing more citizens into them.

Richard worked with a local committee in supervising the construction of a seven-classroom school building. He aided other committees concerned with building courts for volleyball and basketball. He organized a dramatic production given to raise money for landscaping the plaza. He assisted in a project in which the people planted ten thousand small trees on bare mountainsides to prevent erosion.

Richard enlisted the help of Heifer Project. He wanted to start adults raising chickens, and to organize a 4-F Club whose members would raise rabbits and pigeons. We asked Richard, a city-reared lad, if he knew how to handle chickens. His reply provided an insight into one aspect of successful community development. Pointing to a pile of books, Richard said, "I didn't know before I came here, but I am studying about chicken raising and I'm learning."

Willie Heurich was another volunteer with many tails to his kite. He was sent to Ambato to co-ordinate the local contribution to the building of an addition to a schoolhouse. This was no small task because the contribution took several forms. Each family in the school district provided a bag of cement. The town furnished rock, sand, gravel, a bulldozer, and skilled labor. Two volunteer workers a day and occasionally a large number of volunteers were provided for unskilled labor.

The organization of the local contribution was not enough, however, to keep Willie busy. He also taught English in the morning to young people and in the evening to adults. He worked with an Ecuadorian doctor on a plan to set up a rural health project and assisted a local woman in securing a hostel for porters. These burden-bearers, who hire themselves out to carry goods on their backs from one town to another, often sleep in the parks or on the streets because they are too poor to pay for lodging in hotels.

John Binford exhibited the ability to evaluate his own efforts, an asset to any volunteer. John was assigned to school construction and did effective work in this field in two villages, but he was more interested in community development.

While on a construction project where much of the work had to be done by minga labor, John was able to borrow, for a short time, a piece of power machinery. John reported that when the power machinery was no longer available, the people were less willing than before to do by hand the hard labor necessary to complete the job. He had discovered that human nature is the same in Ecuador as in the United States.

While John worked in Los Andes his father paid him a visit. They were both distressed at the sight of the women cooking in their small adobe-walled houses on open fires. Because the houses had no chimneys they were smoke-filled. The smoke so irritated the women's eyes that they were sometimes called "the weeping ones." John and his father planned and built for one of the village families a chimney and an earth stove. The chimney drew well, the stove heated, and the food cooked. The house was free of smoke and "the weeping one" wore a smile, but not for long. John soon found her again cooking on an open fire, her pot resting as before on three stones, her eyes filled with tears. She explained that the stove required much more wood than the open fire, far more than could be obtained in barren Los Andes.

"The people in Llacas did not want a new schoolhouse," Ed Delci said, "but I talked up a trip to a neighboring village where a new schoolhouse had been built. We finally got two busloads to go. When the people saw the newly completed school there, they wanted a schoolhouse too."

When we visited the old schoolhouses we had no doubt of the need for a new building. The boy's school, for example, had five grades, housed in two rooms, one above the other, with the upper room reached by an outside stairway. The rooms, each about twelve by fifteen feet in size, had no windows, making it necessary to keep the doors open for light and air. Fifty-seven pupils in grades one and five were housed in one room, the older pupils seated on crude benches, the small children on the floor. Grades two, three, and four, totaling nearly as many pupils, used the other room. There were in each room a small blackboard, a map, and a few charts made by the teachers. There were no texts for the pupils, only notebooks into which they copied all facts presented so these could be memorized. There was neither a playground nor toilet facilities.

The new school, which replaced both the boys' and girls' schools, was situated on a site high above the village. It was a six-room building of concrete-block construction. Toilet rooms outside the main building were equipped with flush toilets that used water brought down the mountain. Skilled workmen were hired to do the building but mingas were held to collect the rocks for the foundation and perform certain other tasks. From 100 to 125 people turned out for each minga. Ed reported that the women who made up a large part of his labor force were good workers. They came readily and carried heavy loads of rock collected in the valley up the hill to the site of the new building. There were a few parents, however, who were not inclined to work. When the word went out that all school patrons were expected to help at the mingas, twenty children were withdrawn from school.

A local teacher gave excellent leadership in the community. He and Ed helped the people organize committees that assumed various responsibilities. Plans for future community development called for road improvement, painting of houses, and erection of signs.

Some of the landowners in Ecuador have taken steps to end the feudal system prevailing on their haciendas. One such hacendado is Jose Maria Plaza Lasso. At his hacienda on the Plains of Callo he gave to the head of each family attached to the hacienda two and a half hectares (about six acres) of land. At the same time the men were freed from the requirement that they must work for the landowner and those who chose to work on the hacienda were assured of regular wages. By Señor Plaza's act the eighty-six huasipungueros on his hacienda became *libre*, or free men.

Señor Plaza co-operated with certain Ecuadorian and international agencies in developing a housing project at San Augustin de Callo which was intended to improve the living conditions of the workers, nearly all of whom were Indians. A plan for a village was laid out on the plain. The plan called for a community center at the heart of the village. The Indians had always lived in round, one-room huts made of the grass growing on the plains. The houses in the new development were built of concrete blocks, but they retained the thatched roof familiar to the Indians.

A model house was built to show what was to be done. This house, which had five small rooms, was not entirely pleasing to Indian women accustomed to one large room. However, the house with its whitewashed walls and several windows provided more light, air, and cleanliness than the grass huts. The construction of the houses was done with pooled labor, each man working on the building one week out of eight. In addition to erecting a community center and houses, the plan called for the construction of schools and sanitary facilities, and the provision for recreational needs.

Bob Agro and Bill Vickers were Peace Corps volunteers assigned to San Augustin. They gave direction to the self-help housing efforts, taught the Indians to play soccer, and studied the special problems arising from the transition of the Indians from a familiar to a new pattern of community life.

In Ecuador there are thousands of acres of high grass-covered tableland, called the *paramo*, which are not put to any use. The paramo is often damp and cold. The Centro de Reconversión Económica set up an experiment to determine if such land could be made useful. Centro secured a tract on the paramo in southern Ecuador and organized a co-operative among the Indians to raise animals and grow crops. Two Peace Corps volunteers were assigned to the project.

The Indians and the two volunteers built four mud-walled houses in which to live and a barn to shelter sheep. Both houses and barn were roofed with thatch made from the tall grass on the paramo. The men built and stocked duck ponds and rabbit hutches. They planted potatoes, cabbages, and grain. Centro bought a flock of purebred Corriedale sheep. These were placed in the care of Tom Stammer, a volunteer.

As the months wore on the experiment provided some evidence about the usefulness of the paramo. The potatoes were killed by frost, but the cabbages did well. The grass on the paramo did not prove to be nutritious for the sheep and constant dampness caused them to become victims of diseases and parasites. Tom held up well in spite of cold, rainy weather, but the sheep had to be taken to lower ground. Tom and the sheep found a new base near Cuenca where the sheep recovered from their ailments and produced excellent clippings of wool.

It had been shown that sheep raising on the paramo was not successful. But the experiment was continued in order to determine if grains and small animals could be successfully produced on the chilly tablelands of Ecuador.

Cochapata is a remote village in the southern Sierra region of Ecuador. We drove there from Cuenca in a jeep, bumping for three hours over roads that were sometimes fair, more often poor, and in some stretches merely rutted trails.

Cochapata lies in a region where the rainfall is seldom adequate to supply the needs of the cornfields. Centro responded to the plea of the natives for help in securing water. With the aid of two Peace Corps volunteers who are engineers, Centro developed a plan to irrigate the thirsty land.

The two volunteers laid out the route of the ditch that would carry the water some thirty kilometers (about twenty miles) from its source in the mountains to the fields around the village. They set stakes every ten meters (thirty-two and a half feet) to mark each family's monthly quota for digging. The ditch was to be 1 meter (thirty-nine inches) deep and one meter wide.

Centro provided an engineer for consultation and inspection and certain necessary funds. The people of Cochapata undertook to dig the ditch, a task expected to extend over two years. The Peace Corps provided a volunteer to oversee the project. Stanley Laser, one of the young volunteer engineers who laid out the route of the ditch, extended his Peace Corps service to see the project to conclusion.

The plan for digging called for holding a minga each month.

It was agreed that each family must dig at least a ten-meter length at each minga. The length to be dug increased beyond ten meters in proportion to the amount of land owned by a family.

We made the trip to Cochapata on the July day in 1964 when the digging was officially begun with the holding of the first minga. We found five hundred men, women, and children stretched out in a colorful line along the lower route of the ditch. Each family carried its own tools. The first step in the digging was to loosen the hard-packed earth. To do this, a worker, usually a man, lifted a long-handled tool with a blade on the end and brought it down with a blow that thrust the blade into the earth. Then the shovelers fell to, tossing shovelful after shovelful of the loosened earth out of the ditch. The shovelers were often women and sometimes children.

The process went on, loosening and shoveling, loosening and shoveling, through long, weary hours until the family quota for the first minga was completed. After that would come twenty-three other mingas.

One day water will flow through the ditch, corn will grow in the fields, and the people of Cochapata will rejoice. When that time comes the sturdy men and women of the village will have the satisfaction of knowing that with their own strong arms and staunch determination they brought this miracle to pass.

Growing Through Sports and Study

"You can't cheat the stop watch."

In this crisp remark Judy Mucha summed up her convictions that a sports program has great value in Ecuador. The young Peace Corps volunteer saw such a program as a means of building character. She was putting her belief into practice as she directed a large swimming program in Guayaquil. A part of her time in this program was spent in coaching swimmers for matches. Judy believed that such competition was important because of what it did for the swimmers.

"Competition gives the incentive for hard training," Judy explained, "and when a swimmer wins after he has worked hard he knows that honest effort is rewarded. His experience has given him training in integrity."

Swimming is a sport in which all classes in Ecuador participate. Winners in swimming matches are given public praise, regardless of their backgrounds. Judy Mucha saw in this another value of the swimming program. As she put it, " 'Open to all' means training in equality and that is much needed in Ecuador."

Judy's enthusiasm for swimming was a natural product of her own environment and experience. Her mother was a swimmer in the Olympics. Judy swam competitively in AAU (Amateur Athletic Union) meets and was herself a winner several times. When she spoke of the values learned through training she spoke out of hard-won experience.

One of Judy's first projects in Guayaquil was to arrange, with the help of local school officials and sports leaders, for all the children eight to twelve years of age in one district to have a swimming test. On the appointed day 970 children reported to the Municipal Pool.

Since time did not permit Judy to teach all the children to swim, she selected 158 children who could float to form the first swimming class. She taught these children three times a week for three weeks and all learned to swim. The next goal she set was for each child to swim fifty meters. Then came matches to determine the champions of each school in the district. From these champions she selected members for the Alligators. These were teams, one for boys and one for girls, to which she gave special coaching. In her handling of this project Judy put into practice her conviction that competition and the training it inspires are powerful forces in developing individuals.

Building on her success in the first large swimming project, Judy planned to carry out the same program in all other Guayaquil schools, both public and private. She also conducted classes to teach swimming teachers and coaches more effective methods. She taught life-saving classes and tried to have life guards stationed at all swimming sites. Judy continued to coach not only the Alligators but national swimming teams as well. Every day and many evenings Judy Mucha could be found at one or the other of Guayaquil's pools, stop watch in hand, helping young people to become champions and good citizens.

Sports are popular in Ecuador. In a number of cities there are sports federations. Judy Mucha worked with the Guayaquil Sports Federation, the strongest federation in the country. The Peace Corps has taken the position that the values derived from sports justify the use of volunteers in the program.

Dan Roble, a physical education major, also worked with the Guayaquil Sports Federation. His assignment was to work in the recreation program at the Episcopal Center and to help coach sports each afternoon in a local secondary school.

Because of classroom shortages, the boys in the neighborhood

Volunteer Douglas Hinkel teaches physical education in Guayaquil.

of the Episcopal Center attended school only in the afternoons. By eight o'clock each morning thirty-five or forty boys were ready to play games under Dan's direction. They had a choice, for they could play ping-pong and checkers in the center, volley-ball in the backyard, or kickball on an outdoor court a block away. Dan told us that he had placed all the balls in the boys' care. They took turns with this responsibility, each boy serving for one week. He added, "And not one ball has been lost since the boys took charge."

We watched the lithe young lads darting back and forth across the court in a fast game of kickball and admired their skill. They were well on their way toward mastery of the game that engages most of the men of Ecuador in joyous activity.

It was interest in kickball, a form of soccer, that led the men to organize, under Dan's leadership, a ten-team league. Each

paid ten sucres (about sixty cents) per month as his membership fee in the league. Three match games were played each
week, two in the evenings and one on Sunday. The men played
on the same court used by the boys in the mornings. The games
were lively contests with two or three hundred spectators, each
cheering his favorite team.

"In a sense every Peace Corps volunteer in Ecuador is teaching." The deputy director, Mr. Erich Hofmann, made this
comment in discussing the purposes of the Peace Corps program in the country. We understood this statement when we
watched volunteers at work. The basic element in the wide
variety of programs in which they were engaged was instruction, though this was often accomplished by indirect methods.
There were, however, a considerable number of volunteers
whose primary assignment was teaching.

"Everybody in Ecuador wants to study English," Linda
Jewert said, and the prevalence of adult classes in English was
evidence that studying English was very much the vogue, especially in the cities. Linda Jewert taught a full schedule of
English classes at Community Center Number One in Guayaquil, where a well-developed program in adult education was in
progress. The teaching program at this Center was more struc-
tured than was usual in community centers, so volunteers working there had teaching situations somewhat similar to those in
schools. However, the work at the Center was an aspect of
community development, reflecting the conviction of the
Center's director that adult education is the key to community
development.

Jim Galloway taught English at the University of Guayaquil,
and worked with English teachers in the city's largest secondary
school. In the latter assignment he worked from class to class.
He helped to improve the accuracy of spoken English and demonstrated useful methods that the Ecuadorian teachers could

utilize in their own instruction. Jim also taught an English class for adults.

The students who were present one day when we visited Jim's late afternoon class in the Faculty of Chemical Engineering at the University displayed interest and participated readily in the lively exercises that Jim employed to teach spoken and written English.

Joe Enright was assigned in Guayaquil to university teaching, but he was substantially occupied with programs at the Santo Tomás de Aquino School. This private school conducted a six-grade elementary program during the day with seventy pupils enrolled. The school, located in a low-middle-class neighborhood, was housed in three overcrowded upstairs rooms reached by a dark, dangerous stairway. It had meager equipment. In spite of these physical shortcomings the school was aglow with enthusiasm for learning, created by a devoted director and corps of teachers.

Santo Tomás also had an evening program well attended by teen-agers and adults. Classes were given in literacy, English, cooking, sewing, and nursing. Joe Enright taught literacy and English classes in the evening program.

The school was a center in the nutrition program sponsored by Hope Ship. Joe was the director of the Santo Tomás Nutrition Center. Under his guidance women volunteers attended training sessions held at the school and made family visits to check mothers and babies served by this program.

We went with Joe and a nutrition volunteer into a small courtyard around which twenty families lived in one- and two-room apartments. The courtyard was a busy center of activity. The one toilet and the one water spigot that served all the families were located there. The women washed in the courtyard in low wooden tubs, scrubbing their clothes in cold water with stiff brushes. Children played about in the clutter. Chickens, cats, and dogs searched for stray bites of food.

Volunteers teaching in Ecuador served in a variety of situations. Alice Harris taught music at the Legión Femenina de Educación Popular, a private school in Guayaquil with a good building and adequate equipment. Richard Schroeder taught Braille at the School for the Blind in Guayaquil. Roberta Lobbin taught a course in design for Indian weavers and a course in ceramics for Indian potterymakers in the area near Riobamba. Both courses were given to help native craftsmen improve the quality of their products so these would sell more readily. Douglas Reid set up a silk-screening shop in the School of Work, a correctional school for boys in Guayaquil. Douglas taught the boys the silk-screening technique for printing, and reproducing designs. George Staton taught English at Catholic University, counseled at the Girl's Reform School, and gave therapy at a local mental hospital. George and Douglas Reid also co-operated in organizing a Boy's Club in Guayaquil. The club program included both formal and informal teaching.

Sarah Sunkel, better known as Susie, was assigned to teach English in the Normal School at Baños, Tungurahua Province. Arriving during the school vacation, Susie started at once to teach three adult English classes. Earlier volunteers in Baños had worked with leaders in the town to secure a community center. The plans made by the group called for renting a building to serve as a center, and for conducting, at the center, a program of recreation and adult education.

Susie gave enthusiastic support to these plans. She had confidence in the benefits that teaching could bring to the Ecuadorians. "They need self-assurance," she observed.

In these words Susie Sunkel expressed the real purpose of the teaching program, perhaps of the total Peace Corps effort in Ecuador. For it is a program aimed at helping Ecuadorians to acquire the knowledge and skills by means of which they can help themselves and thus gain the self-assurance necessary to successful living.

3. AT WORK IN SIERRA LEONE

Mountain of the Lion

Sierra Leone is a land of burden-bearers. In the cities, as well as in the up-country, men, women, and children glide along with loads on their heads. The burden may weigh many pounds or it may be as easily spilled as a dish of soup, but it is transported on the head. This form of burden-bearing is only one example of the primitive state of life that generally prevails in Sierra Leone. However, the nation is struggling to change its ancient patterns of living, to find better ways to meet its daily needs. Sierra Leone has very far to go. Some of its efforts are feeble, but the nation has made a beginning.

In Sierra Leone the bush wages an eternal struggle with man for possession of the land. This constant encroachment of vegetation is due to climatic conditions. The rain, which falls largely through a period of eight or nine months, amounts to about 150 inches per year. During the period from December to March hot, dry winds blow and the dust swirls. The temperature, which is high, changes very little from one month to another, but it is hotter along the coast than in the interior, where elevation gives some relief from heat and humidity. Such climatic conditions favor lush plant growth.

Sierra Leone is only a little larger than West Virginia. It stretches for about 210 miles along the Atlantic Coast of West Africa and reaches inland some 180 miles. Its neighbors are Guinea on the north and Liberia on the east. A low, flat coast, once forest-covered, is broken by wide-mouthed rivers flowing into the ocean. Rising abruptly from the coastal plain is a plateau averaging fifteen hundred feet in elevation. Here and there are mountain peaks reaching much higher.

The coast was visited by Portuguese navigators in search of a new route to the Indies. One of the navigators is said to have given a peninsula along the coast the name that became the name of the country. The words "Sierra Leone" mean literally "mountain lion." Some people believe that the Portuguese sailors thought the mountains rising behind the coast resembled crouching lions. Others hold that the roll of thunder echoing through the mountains during storms sounded like the roaring of lions.

Freetown, the capital of Sierra Leone, is on the south bank of the broad, deep estuary of the Sierra Leone River. The harbor formed by the estuary is one of the largest natural harbors in the world. The international airport is across the harbor from Freetown. The airport is reached by ferry.

European traders, pirates, and missionaries visited the coast of Sierra Leone after its discovery, and some trading posts were established there. In 1787 a group of settlers, most of whom were former Negro slaves who had been granted their freedom, arrived from England and settled on the site of present-day Freetown. In 1792 a large party of freed Negroes went from Nova Scotia to join the settlement at Freetown. In 1808 the settlement was made a British Crown Colony, with a governor appointed as the representative of the British ruler.

Later settlers arrived in Freetown when British naval vessels stopped slave ships of other nations, took off the captive Negroes aboard, and carried them to Freetown, where they were set free. These arrivals were called recaptives because they had twice been made captives.

The earlier settlers developed a sense of identity as one people, who came to be known as Creoles. At first the earlier settlers refused to accept the recaptives as their equals, or as Creoles, but time blurred old differences and the name Creole finally came to be applied to all the people in the Crown Colony.

The Creoles spoke English, but gradually a new language called Krio developed in the Colony. Krio was derived from the several tongues spoken along the West African Coast.

The Creoles welcomed missionaries and established churches in the Colony. They started schools and in 1827 established Fourah Bay College, which for many years was the center of education in West Africa.

The values cherished by the Creoles led them to make notable advances, but unfortunately, they developed a strong sense of superiority to the Negroes living outside the Colony. This attitude affected their relations with their neighbors.

In 1896 Britain declared its authority over an area bordering the Crown Colony. Because the British stated their purpose to be the protection of the area, it was called the Protectorate. For many years the British governed the Protectorate separately from the Crown Colony, but in 1951 the British merged the Colony and the Protectorate under one government. Each area was given representation in the lawmaking body, but because the Protectorate was larger and more populous it had the larger number of representatives. The Colony bitterly resented this situation.

The leader who emerged in the new joint government was Dr. Milton Margai. He was a man from the Protectorate but he did much to bridge the differences that existed between the people of the Colony and the people of the Protectorate.

Dr. Margai led Sierra Leone in preparing for independence, which Britain proved willing to grant. On April 27, 1961, Sierra Leone became an independent nation, made up of four provinces. The head of the government is the Premier. Dr. Milton Margai became the first premier of the new nation.

Sierra Leone has about two and a half million people, most of whom are Negroes. Tribal organization is the normal manner of living among the Negroes of tropical Africa. In Sierra Leone there are thirteen tribes, but about 60 per cent of the people belong to the two larger tribes, the Mende and the Temne. The Creoles today, descendants of the freed slaves who settled Freetown, are normally outside the tribal organization.

Each tribe in Sierra Leone is divided into a number of units or chiefdoms. The people in the chiefdom choose, from among those eligible to serve, the head of the chiefdom, who is called the Paramount Chief. Assisting him in administering certain local matters is the Chiefdom Council, over which the Paramount Chief presides. The administration of tribal officials is subject to the authority of the central government.

The tribes speak their tribal languages. Many also speak a dialect called Mandinka, which is a combination of Mende and Temne. The Creoles speak Krio. The official language is English, which is taught in the schools and spoken by a considerable number, though not all, of the people.

There are Christians, Moslems, and followers of native African religions in Sierra Leone. The people do not usually have conflicts over their differing beliefs.

Secret societies play a part in tribal life. Each secret society has its own rituals and ceremonies.

Agriculture is the principal occupation in Sierra Leone but much of it is no more than subsistence farming. The food crops thus raised include rice, millet, sorghum, cassava, sweet potatoes, and peanuts, which are called ground nuts in Sierra Leone. The main agricultural product for export is palm kernels. Coffee, cacao, piassava, and ginger are exported in small quantities.

The very heavy rains wash out of the soil elements needed for plant growth. Another serious handicap to agriculture is the lack of power with which to carry on farm operations. The bite of the tsetse fly, which is a prevalent insect in Sierra Leone, causes paralysis in horses and cows. The coastal region is more seriously affected than the uplands, but nowhere in the country is there an adequate supply of draft animals. Most farming is on too small a scale to use power equipment and most farmers are too poor to afford such equipment. The farm work is done largely by women, using short-handled hoes and machetes.

Sierra Leone has some valuable minerals. Among these are rutile and ilmenite, from which titanium is extracted, chromite, bauxite, iron, and diamonds. The latter include both industrial diamonds and gem stones.

The richest diamond deposit found is in the Bafi-Sewa River drainage system, where the stones are imbedded in gravel. The diamonds are mined by digging out the gravel beds and washing away the waste. The production and sale of diamonds provides the greatest single source of revenue in the country.

Sierra Leone needs roads and the government is pushing construction. Trucks, called lorries in Sierra Leone, are much used to transport both goods and people.

Sierra Leone has set for itself the long-range goal of free, compulsory primary education. It has increased the support for secondary schools. Fourah Bay College has been transformed on a new campus into the University College of Sierra Leone. Students have been sent abroad to study on government scholarships. Teachers from the American Peace Corps and other national service corps have been invited to help staff Sierra Leone schools.

These efforts to improve education are significant because they touch the heart of the nation's problem. If Sierra Leone is to be transformed from a primitive to an advanced nation, the people must understand the values to be gained by exchanging an old way of life for a new way. And they must understand the price, in terms of human effort, that has to be paid for such transformation. Understanding such as this comes only through education.

We flew into the airport at Freetown in the early morning of a day that proved to be hot and humid. Because of a long delay at the ferry it was almost noon when we reached the hotel where we had confirmed reservations. We were weary after an overnight flight but sustained by thought of the comfort of an air-conditioned room. At the hotel we learned that our reservations were canceled. An official party, larger than expected, had arrived from a neighboring country and occupied all the hotel rooms.

Mr. Donovan McClure, Director of the Peace Corps for Sierra Leone, came to our rescue and found us overnight accommodations. The next day we were off in a Peace Corps jeep to see volunteers working in the interior of the country. When we returned to Freetown, after some days, during which we stayed in the homes of volunteers and in the guest house of a diamond-mining company, the official party had departed and we were received as guests at Freetown's best hotel.

Widening Horizons in Sierra Leone

It was New Year's Day, 1964. In Jimmi Bagbo a feast was spread. A group of sturdy Peace Corps volunteers did full justice to it, while their host, Paramount Chief Raymond B. S. Koker, beamed. When the volunteers were filled with African delicacies they found seats around the Chief's compound.

"Bong! Bong! Bong!"

The sound of the drums brought the volunteers out of their after-dinner lethargy as a line of dancers pranced into the compound and broke into a tribal dance. This was the beginning of the program of entertainment arranged by the Paramount Chief for his guests, but it was not the end. Rumor said that the Chief had planned a surprise to climax the entertainment. Everyone was alert, watching the entrance to the compound.

Then it came, a figure costumed and masked, a devil dressed in raffia. As recognition of the significance of the mask and costume spread, a murmur ran through the room—"a Poro devil!" Every eye was fixed on the devil as he went through the steps of the Poro Society ritual dance. This was indeed a surprise, and a great honor to the Peace Corps volunteers, too, for this was but the third appearance in seven years of the devil from the famous secret society.

The Paramount Chief's feast and entertainment were an expression of the gratitude he felt to the volunteers who had given the week between Christmas and New Year's to help the village build a school library. From their assignments in various parts of Sierra Leone, volunteers had gone to Jimmi Bagbo during school vacation to join the volunteers stationed there. Together, the visitors and the resident volunteers had made mud bricks and poured cement. Now the building to house the library was well on its way. With the feasting and entertainment ended, the visiting volunteers prepared to return to their own assignments. Before they were gone they were to receive a final expression of appreciation, this one from the Honorable John H. Tucker, member of the Sierra Leone Parliament from Jimmi Bagbo. The right honorable member said, "If you people can come and build a school library for us, then certainly we can do the same. We thank you for showing us how to help ourselves."

Peter and Rosalie Williams, two of the volunteers who were involved in the library-building project, were teachers at the Boys' Secondary School in Jimmi Bagbo. Peter taught general science and mathematics, Rosalie taught English. The school extended only through the third form, which is about equal to the tenth grade in the United States.

The young volunteers were enthusiastic about their teaching, but it proved to be only the starting point in their work at Jimmi Bagbo. Soon after their arrival in the community, Peter planted a garden. Then, impressed by the inadequate diet of the natives, he built a chicken house and bought 110 baby chicks from the government hatchery.

When his hens began to lay, six to seven months later, Peter had eggs to sell. The price of eggs in Jimmi Bagbo was one dollar per dozen. Peter sold his eggs for half that amount, for his purpose was not profit. He wanted to make eggs available for food, especially for certain undernourished children. He also wanted to encourage native families to start raising chickens. For those who would do so he provided fertile eggs at reasonable cost. Then, as more natives became interested in chicken raising, Peter sold his chickens at cost to provide breed-

Tim Howell gives a young friend in Sierra Leone a ride.

ing stock. He and Rosalie secured a new lot of baby chicks and started a second project, again showing by example how the people of Jimmi Bagbo could improve their nutrition.

Wells were needed in Jimmi Bagbo. A volunteer in the rural development program gave advice, Peter gave leadership, men of the town under orders of the Paramount Chief provided labor, CARE donated a pump, and a community well was built. Inspired by their success, the men also put down a well to supply water for the school.

The library building was finished and books donated by volunteers and the English Speaking Union were received. Peter and Rosalie co-operated with Paramount Chief Koker, a man of influence in Sierra Leone, in his efforts to lift the level of life in Jimmi Bagbo. The young volunteers taught a Sunday school class in the local church. They gave attention to helping boys learn the value of truthfulness and integrity. In the several ways open to them in Jimmi Bagbo, Peter and Rosalie Williams kindled the spark.

Three young women volunteers taught in the Girls' Secondary School, a government boarding school, at Magburaka. Mary Haak taught health education and domestic science (home economics), Barbara Hoffman taught science, and Gay Revi taught English.

The girls lived together in a comfortable apartment. The teacher residences, each a two-family building, stood in a group at the edge of the school campus. Around each house was a strip kept completely bare of the ever-encroaching grass, as a protection against snakes. This device was not wholly successful. Snakes occasionally crawled into the houses, but the natives of Sierra Leone, who generally practice the same precaution, believe that snakes are less likely to cross bare earth than to crawl through grass.

The school at Magburaka, the only girls' boarding school up-country, is newly established. Its buildings, of tropical design, are attractive and adequate. There are two classroom and laboratory buildings, an office, a dining hall and kitchen, and several dormitories on the large campus, or compound. This is a better educational plant than is usual in Sierra Leone.

The students, who go to Magburaka from all over the country, live in the dormitories in groups of about fifteen. They pay tuition, as do all students in all schools, both primary and secondary, in Sierra Leone, but the tuition is not high at Magburaka. The school offers work through the fifth form. This is about equivalent to our twelfth grade.

The volunteers teaching at Magburaka found their laboratories well equipped. The domestic science kitchens in which Mary's classes learned cooking had elaborate equipment donated by CARE, but it seemed unlikely that many of the students would ever have such equipment in their homes.

Though well equipped, the school lacked adequate funds for current expenses. This shortage led to a lack of textbooks which the teachers found to be a serious handicap. There was also a shortage of money to buy food for the cooking classes. It was expected that the small sum budgeted for this purpose would be replaced through sale of the cooked food to the girls, a demand that Mary found frustrating.

The school system, as in all schools in Sierra Leone, was formal. Because of the great importance attached to passing examinations the students were encouraged to take elaborate notes and memorize them. The shortage of books made this more necessary.

The students sometimes had arguments outside of class, when they yelled and screamed at each other, but they behaved well in class. There was no recreation program, nor much contact outside of class between teachers and pupils. Mary, Barbara, and Gay were concerned about this and made an effort to get acquainted with the students as individuals.

They played netball with the girls, talked to them, and now and then invited the girls to their apartment. They were shocked when the girls first came as their guests to have them go to their back door. This, it seemed, was a custom established in colonial days. The Peace Corps volunteers promptly ended that remnant of colonialism and taught a lesson in democracy by assuring the students that they expected all their guests to enter through the front door.

What would your day be like if you attended a secondary boarding school in Sierra Leone?

At the Government Secondary School in Kenema where one half or more of the boys are boarding students, you would rise at six-fifty, and after breakfast and morning chores, report to the dining hall at eight A.M. for opening exercises, followed by marking of attendance. From eight-twenty to ten-twenty you would attend three forty-minute classes, after which you would have a ten-minute break, and then report to two more classes. After lunch you would have two classes, with dismissal at 2 P.M. By this time, with tropical heat prevailing, you would probably need the hour of freedom provided in the schedule. You would be expected, but not required, to study from three until five o'clock and to take part in sports from five until seven o'clock. After an hour for dinner, you would report to classrooms for required, supervised study from 8 until 10:30 P.M. A quick run to the dormitories would end your day and allow lights out as required at 10:45 P.M.

The school at Kenema has five forms with some three hundred students enrolled, about half of whom are boarding students living in dormitories on the campus. The dozen girls in the student body and the remainder of the boys live in the community, either in their own homes or with friends.

The school has generally been understaffed, even with the help of nationals from England and Canada and from the

American Peace Corps. Four volunteers who worked in the school were Walt Barrow, who taught history and geography, Marcia Watkins in English, Martha Peters in history and French, and Don Harris, who taught mathematics and science.

Houses for teachers are provided on the campus. Don and Walt lived in a comfortable two-bedroom house, which was managed by their steward, Timmie, who had a houseboy to help him. Marcia and Martha lived together in a similar house, but they prepared their own meals.

The volunteers found the school library fairly adequate, but the students lacked broad interests and rarely used the library for other than assigned reading. Textbooks were available in some classes, but not in all, which was a serious lack. Students did all their written work in exercise books which, when handed in, had to be returned by the teacher the next day. The students here, as in other schools in Sierra Leone, were concerned principally with memorizing in order to pass external examinations. It is of interest to know that even though the volunteers have been trained in a different system, the students that they teach do pass their examinations.

Walt Barrows, in his second year of teaching at the school, found reason to believe that student learning could be extended beyond mere memorization. His new students still wanted to do rote learning, but the students that he had taught the year before were willing to enter into discussion and could use the facts they had learned as a basis for reasoning about problems encountered.

Walt also served as sports master. He reported that the boys usually went out for sports. They enjoyed match games of soccer and cricket and participated in field meets.

Marcia Watkins sponsored a literary society which met every other Friday evening. At the meetings, the members waxed eloquent in speeches and debates and developed a skill often used among Africans, who favor what they call "palaver."

The students at Kenema were reasonably well behaved, but

the boys enjoyed a little mischief and were as capable as American boys of diverting the teacher from the lesson. In a chemistry class Don Harris explained the structure and properties of liquids. When he asked for questions a boy raised his hand.

"Why does the sugar in my teacup become hard when I pour milk and hot tea on it?" the boy asked.

"I have never seen this happen," Don replied.

Whereupon, the boy insisted, with enough elaborations to consume the remainder of the class period, that the phenomenon did indeed happen. When the bell rang, Don said, "We shall try an experiment and see what happens to the sugar."

As I rose to leave, I said, "I am sorry that I shall not be here to see *that* experiment."

The boys in the class, who had been smiling broadly while their classmate used up the period, burst into laughter.

James and Gloria Wilson, bride and groom as well as Peace Corps volunteers, arrived in Yengema to teach in a small, new Secondary School for Boys operated by a Roman Catholic Mission. The house which was to serve as their first home was a five-room, mud-walled structure, roofed in corrugated metal and floored with a mixture of sand and cement which yielded a cup of sand at each sweeping. The cement plaster, inside and out, was painted pink with black trim. The windows had iron bars and wooden shutters but no glass. Water for all household purposes came from the rain barrel in the rainy season and was carried from a neighbor's well in the dry season. The house was lighted by kerosene lamps. Sanitary needs were provided for by an outdoor latrine.

The new schoolhouse was a concrete-block structure plastered with cement and provided with outdoor latrines. The ninety boys who filled the three classrooms were neatly dressed, with every boy wearing a clean white shirt.

A Catholic priest attached to the mission served as principal

and taught languages and religion. James and Gloria, who are
Protestants, had no part in religious instruction. James taught
general science, mathematics, and English literature. Gloria
taught history, geography, literature, and reading. Gloria directed the school chorus and James helped coach the four
athletic teams organized within the school. The young volunteers hoped to draw upon their own interests in crafts, dramatics, and science to provide the basis for school clubs.

Yengema, a small town, is the center of operations for the
Sierra Leone Selection Trust, Ltd., the country's leading diamond-mining corporation. The presence of the company brings
to the community more skilled and educated Africans than
might otherwise be found in a town the size of Yengema. James
and Gloria were well received by these staff members. The
principal of the primary school, a leader in the community,
extended cordial hospitality to the young couple. The priests
attached to the Catholic mission and the leaders of the town's
Protestant church, the Evangelical United Brethren, welcomed
the volunteers.

James and Gloria faced numerous challenges in their Peace
Corps service. Newly married, teaching for the first time, adjusting to life in the tropics, learning to live without modern
conveniences, finding a place in the social structure of an unfamiliar environment were all experiences that tested them.
But James and Gloria Wilson met the test successfully.

Certain volunteers were assigned to the Ministry of Education and placed in very specialized types of work. Birge Al-
bright worked with the Chief Justice in codifying laws. John
Gray gave assistance in preparing programs for the Sierra
Leone Television Station. Ethel Hill, Joan Loslo, and Lon Dick-
erson worked under the direction of the Library Board. Janet
Stone was the curator of the Sierra Leone Museum.

Ethel Hill and Joan Loslo were trained librarians. Lon Dick-erson had had only practical experience in a library. The three worked at various undertakings as directed by the Chief of the National Library. Their activities included cataloguing books, organizing United Nations documents at the National Library, and organizing and cataloguing at the library of the Technical Institute. Both of these institutions are in Freetown.

Joan's assignment was to continue in Freetown. Ethel Hill expected to go later to Njala University to lend technical aid in the library there. Lon was eager to begin his assignment to go on a bookmobile. This work would take him into the tribal villages where he would have the opportunity to introduce books to people who had had only meager contact with ideas presented on the printed page.

In the first months of their assignment in Sierra Leone the volunteers had discovered that a strange culture demands certain adjustments. They all missed green, uncooked food, which was avoided because such food was sometimes contaminated due to the way it was grown and handled. Don missed fresh milk. They had discovered that the local people were willing to co-operate but did not always know how to do it. They had had pleasant social gatherings with other volunteers, but only meager contacts with local people.

The three volunteers took the adjustments in stride but they were concerned because no counterparts had been provided to learn library techniques. They were challenged by the library needs of the nation and they wanted to leave trained counterparts to carry on when they left.

Janet Stone was a professionally trained and experienced museum worker before she became a Peace Corps volunteer. Her assignment was to work in the Sierra Leone Museum in Freetown.

The museum has a considerable collection of articles that reflect both the actual life of the people and their cultural heritage. It attracts a constant flow of visitors, who come at the average rate of 180 per hour. The building is crowded with exhibits and people and Janet has already compiled a list of requirements for a new building.

Gary Schulze, a previous Peace Corps volunteer on this job, was not professionally trained, but he added to the collection and did effective publicity work for the museum. Janet has secured and catalogued exhibits, arranged for the display of museum articles at several public buildings in Freetown, provided for the sale of postcards depicting rare exhibits, secured a technician who is in training on the job, developed publicity—in short has moved the Museum forward as a professional institution. Janet's two great frustrations have been lack of funds and lack of interest upon the part of some of the educated people in the country who could be helpful. But she has had rich rewards. She was named Curator of the Museum and in this capacity she was sent to a meeting in Nigeria sponsored by UNESCO, which dealt with the role of museums in contemporary Africa.

"I would do it again," Janet said of her Peace Corps service. She has had deep satisfaction in helping to develop an institution which presents to the people of Sierra Leone a record of their past that may well serve as a challenge to their future accomplishments.

Building for a Better Tomorrow

The tropical sun cast a glare over the dusty, winding streets of Masingbi. By contrast, the Paramount Chief's Council Chamber was shaded and cool. Open at the sides and protected by a thatched roof, this meeting place for the elders of the chiefdom offered a pleasant retreat from the heat.

Paramount Chief Bai Kurri-Kananfoi II ushered us into the dimly lighted meeting place and seated us on chairs. Within minutes a dozen or more men filed in and took seats on benches at one side. Curiosity had quickly fetched a crowd.

The Paramount Chief was a strong, well-built man. He was dressed in freshly laundered white cotton garments—trousers and a tunic that reached to his knees—and yellow shoes. A white turban wrapped about his head presented a startling contrast to the intense blackness of his skin.

The Chief welcomed us and told us about his chiefdom. Though spoken of as "a village," Masingbi has about twenty-three hundred people. The tribal land holdings stretch over a considerable area around the center of settlement in which most of the people live. The Chiefdom Council that serves with the Paramount Chief is made up of eight councilors, most of whom were in the group of men who followed the visitors into the Council Chamber. The Chief used excellent English and spoke in a pleasant voice as he described the chiefdom and his responsibility, with the councilors, for law and order.

Learning that we wished to see the water system being installed for Masingbi, the Paramount Chief led the way up the hill to the storage tank, and then on to see other village improvements. Behind us came a procession of village men and boys. Returning, the Chief insisted that we refresh ourselves in the dim coolness of his Council Chamber. At the Chief's direction, African soft drinks and glasses were brought. The drinks were served to us and to the Chief. We sat and sipped under the unblinking gaze of the curious crowd, which was once more seated on the benches.

Courteous to the end, Paramount Chief Bai Kurri-Kananfoi II accompanied us to the Peace Corps jeep in which we had come. He posed for pictures, but the camera alone could not reveal the full measure of this modern chief, symbol of an old way of African life, yet embodying within his person understanding of today's world and the will to prepare his people to live in that world.

Masingbi was the scene of one of the projects carried out under the Rural Development program that has operated in

Sierra Leone villagers teach volunteer Bill Atkins a new game.

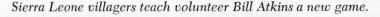

Sierra Leone. Under this program Peace Corps volunteers with skills in construction work assisted with public improvements requested by the chiefs and approved by the proper authorities. Roads, bridges, culverts, schoolhouses, dispensaries, a water system, and a cattle-weighing station were among the public works constructed under the program.

To secure technical direction and oversight for Rural Development the Peace Corps made a contract with CARE. This organization then provided a CARE administrator who had an office in Freetown from which he directed the program. Certain Rural Development men, designated as volunteer leaders, proved useful in co-ordinating the work. Each of the volunteers working in Rural Development usually had several projects underway at the same time.

Housing centers for the young men in Rural Development were established at a dozen or so places in the country. Two or more men used each of the Rural Development houses as a base residence. When the demands of a job made it necessary for a volunteer to remain overnight, or for several nights, near a project, he was usually given a room in the Paramount Chief's house.

Rural Development men had to travel, often to remote places, to do their work, so each had access to a vehicle—a Land-Rover, truck, or jeep—provided by the Sierra Leone government. This provision of vehicles, made necessary by the nature of Rural Development work, was contrary to the Peace Corps policy of curtailing the use of vehicles.

In 1964 the Peace Corps proposed a new plan which was intended eventually to replace its Rural Development program. Three pilot projects were set up to test the new plan. One of the pilot projects was established at Masingbi.

Under the new plan a volunteer lives in each village where improvements are sought. The volunteer gives leadership in the solution of community problems. The activities by which communities are improved varies from village to village, and from time to time within any given village. This is essentially the plan operating in Ecuador, and many other Latin American countries, where it is known as community development, a term which is also to be used in Sierra Leone.

Ken Priebe was the volunteer, under the Rural Development program, who directed the construction of a water system for Masingbi. Ken found a small valley into which water drained from the surrounding hills. In this natural basin Ken had workmen from Masingbi build a reservoir. Water was collected by three lead-in channels where it flowed over layers of stone for filtering. The three channels then led into one large channel where the water passed through three metal screens before entering the reservoir. The channels and reservoir were built of concrete.

The valley which provided the source of the water was separated from Masingbi by a hill. Ken and the workmen built a storage tank on the top of the hill. The tank, sixteen by sixteen by seven feet, held sixteen thousand gallons of water. The water was pumped uphill through pipes from the reservoir to the storage tank. The pump for lifting the water, located on the bank above the reservoir, was donated by CARE.

From the storage tank on the hill, the water ran through pipes down to the village. The Chief ordered fourteen spigots placed at various points in Masingbi so water would be near all the village households. This water system, in operation, was an undreamed-of convenience to the women of Masingbi, upon whom the burden of water-carrying had rested.

Ken Priebe shared a Rural Development residence with two other volunteers. The three young men held their dog, Susie, and her six pups in common ownership and affection, but the other two volunteers gladly left to Ken sole ownership of and responsibility for Kayak, a "putty nose" monkey. The little creature was tiny, weighing perhaps three pounds, but his capacity for bananas and mischief was mighty.

In Sierra Leone the government has established district hospitals, each headed by a doctor. Medical and health services at the local level are rendered by a government dispenser who goes to the villages. A building is needed as a center in which the dispenser can work. In Masingbi the Paramount Chief set men to work molding in a hand-operated machine three thousand cinva blocks to build a dispensary. Louis Rapoport, the volunteer who was going to Masingbi under the new community development plan, expected to be there to help erect the dispensary.

The men of Masingbi, at the direction of the Paramount Chief, built a cutoff road which saved eight miles of travel in reaching the next village. Encouraged by this success and the prospect of a volunteer in residence, the village leaders made plans for improvements to be carried out with Louis Rapoport's help.

High on the list was improvement of farming practices. The village people grew citrus fruit, which was sold in the cities. They grew upland rice to provide food. Their fruit crop suffered because of pests and diseases. Their upland rice, broadcast on poorly prepared ground and soon choked with weeds, yielded only a small crop. Louis Rapoport took a short course at an agricultural training center before he went to Masingbi. He learned how to help the farmers control pests and diseases that attacked their fruit. He was also trained to introduce more efficient ways to prepare soil, to sow rice, and to care for the crop.

Louis and the village leaders hoped to establish literacy classes, provide sanitary facilities, organize a co-operative, build a community center, set up a recreation program, and secure a gas or diesel generator so that moving pictures could be shown in the village, which had no electricity. If even some of these ambitious plans were realized Masingbi would be a different and a better place in which to live.

William Atkins was a bricklayer with some years of experience who became a Peace Corps volunteer. He was stationed at Bo. In his first six months in Sierra Leone, William supervised the construction of a new road, the repairing of another road, and the building of a schoolhouse. The work on these projects was done by men from the communities benefited by the improvements. The plan of working together, or using communal labor, is familiar to the Africans, and is one that they enter into readily.

Jeff Mereck and Mike Dyer were Volunteer Leaders in the Northern Province under the Rural Development Plan. Tim Howell served as Volunteer Leader for both the Southern and Eastern provinces. The three men had similar duties.

The process by which a project was begun and carried to a finish under Rural Development was complicated. It began with a list of needs in a chiefdom submitted by the Chief to his immediate superior in the government, the District Officer. The process involved the CARE Administrator, who had to approve a project before it could go forward, the Volunteer Leader, who checked the availability of funds, and the volunteer who was assigned to give direct supervision to the project. In a country that had neither adequate telephone nor rapid mail communication among the officials involved, the process of setting up a project was slow and often frustrating.

Jeff Mereck was a young man who was determined to join the Peace Corps. The effects of a football injury were for a time a barrier, but Jeff made the Corps in spite of the handicap, and became a successful Volunteer Leader. When the new plan for Community Development was proposed Jeff made a survey of each chiefdom to find its needs and potential. This background information provided a working basis upon which to start Community Development.

Tim Howell was graduated from a university with a degree in architecture and took an office position as an apprentice architect. Energetic, restless Tim was soon bored with what he termed "the nine to five rut." He joined the Peace Corps and became a Volunteer Leader. He liked the freedom of movement, the involvement with people, and the scope for creativity which his Peace Corps job permitted. In doing this job he reached a decision about the type of work he wanted to do in the future. Tim decided that he wanted to establish a firm of his own and thus have an opportunity to develop his ideas in the field of building.

In his Peace Corps experience Tim learned a lesson that may prove useful when he is operating his firm. He discovered that creativity cannot go too far beyond the taste or aesthetic standards of the people that it serves. Tim adapted for a schoolhouse in Neama the plan of an A house, in which the roof slopes to the ground to form the sides of the building. The roof was corrugated metal painted with aluminum paint. The triangular-shaped walls at each end were constructed of native stone, left with a rough, uneven surface.

The cost of a schoolhouse built with the A plan was less than the cost of a building with more conventional construction. The appearance was striking and modern. Moreover, by Tim's standards, the rock walls were beautiful.

Norman Tyler, the volunteer who worked on the project, shared Tim's appreciation of the artistic qualities of the rough, stony surface. Unfortunately the leaders in Neama did not hold the same view. They considered the rough walls unfinished and ugly and refused to be persuaded of their beauty. After much palaver over the matter, Tim and Norman sadly set about the task of applying a coating of cement to both the inside and outside of the stone walls.

Seeking to understand the great value placed by the men of Neama on smooth walls, Norman said, "I believe it is because they have always lived in primitive dwellings. Now that they are trying to improve they want something that looks finished."

Norman Tyler had two years of architectural training before

he left school to join the Peace Corps. He believed that he was gaining valuable experience in his chosen field and he expected to return to the university and complete his training when his tour of duty ended.

Norman appreciated the Africans' sense of humor. He found that the laborers who worked on his projects were natural mimics. When he handled a level, or other tool, he often found an African picking up a stick and with a broad grin imitating his movements.

Norman commented upon the speed with which men doing communal labor often completed their task. He said, "Two hundred men came one day to clean a building site of grass. There was much confusion until a drummer began to beat his drum. Immediately the men lined up in ten lines and as the drummer beat the drum the men moved across the field chopping up

Men in Neama work on the A-frame schoolhouse erected under the direction of Tim Howell and Norman Tyler, Peace Corps volunteers.

grass with their short-handled hoes. That site was cleared in a matter of minutes."

The Peace Corps received a call for a volunteer to set up a program at the Kono Community Center and Ron Hall was given the assignment. The Center, located in Koidu, was built by the Sierra Leone Selection Trust, Ltd. Koidu, a diamond-mining center, has grown rapidly in recent years. The Kono Community Center was opened in January 1964, with ceremonies marked by the presence of the Premier, Sir Milton Margai.

A large recreation and meeting room in the handsome Center is dominated by a mural that covers the entire wall opposite the entrance to the room. The mural, which depicts dancers, medicine men, ceremonial devils and other figures associated with West African life, is informally divided into three panels by pictured palm trees. The mural was painted by a local artist who works as a foreman for the Selection Trust.

One end of the Center is devoted to a library and the opposite end to apartments for the warden and watchman who care for and guard the building. There is a small bar and a room for writing and cards. A playing field adjoins the building.

The Selection Trust provided tables and chairs. The American Embassy donated books and game equipment. The Central Government sent a shipment of books for the library. The District Council provided funds to employ a librarian.

Ron started his work by organizing after-school recreation for youths. About a hundred young people came each day, but true to African custom that keeps the female in the background, these were largely boys. Most of those who came were in school either in Koidu or Yengema. The youths who did not attend school did not usually go to the Community Center, either.

With characteristic enthusiasm, Ron threw himself into a frenzy of program planning for the Center. One result was an eleven-page report that he submitted to the District Officer, who

accepted Ron's plans but needed time to find the means to im-
plement them. The first need was to devise a way to pay the
operating costs of the Center. Beyond that, Ron hoped that the
program would provide wholesome activities for both youths
and adults. He believed that such activities would develop community leaders and create a community spirit, a great need at
the Kona Center. The diamond rush to the Kona District had
brought several thousand new people to the area. Uprooted
from other communities they had no sense of belonging to their
new community.

Ron Hall's purpose was to establish a program that would
meet the needs of the local situation and at the same time serve
as a pilot project for similar programs in other places. Under
the new plan of Community Development in Sierra Leone,
centers will be built in many villages. To show how a community center may become the nucleus of a well-integrated, for-
ward-looking, striving community may well be one of the most
valuable contributions that the Peace Corps can make to Sierra
Leone.

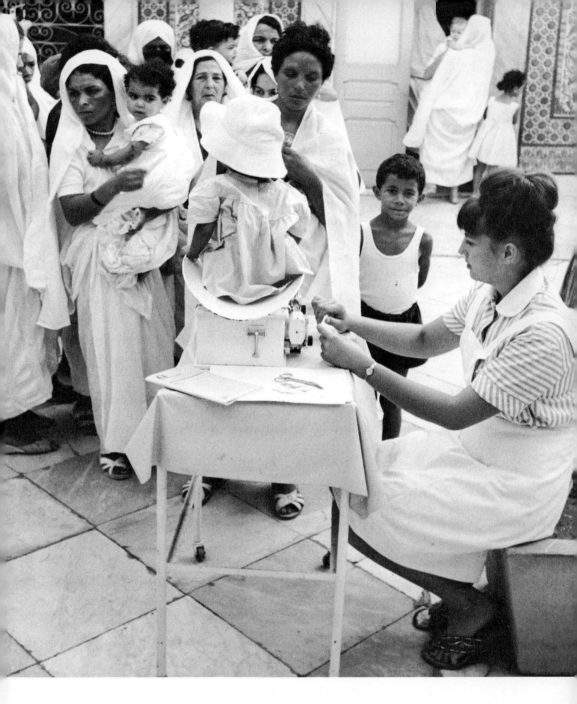

4. AT WORK IN TUNISIA

Nation at the Crossroads

We stood on the hill that caps the peninsula forming one side of the Gulf of Tunis. At our feet lay the harbor, beyond stretched the blue waters of the Mediterranean Sea. Standing thus on Byrsa Hill, we could all but see the tall-masted Phoenician vessels that nearly three thousand years before had put into the harbor seeking safe anchorage and a site for a trading station.

The daring Phoenician sailors came from their home on the eastern shore of the Mediterranean and established settlements on the North African coast. The trading station that they planted on Byrsa Hill prospered and became a city of importance in the ancient world. The city was named Carthage.

In the pattern of the times, Carthage became a powerful city-state and thus a rival of Rome, another rising power. At the end of three bitter wars between the rivals, Carthage was crushed by Rome in 146 B.C. The Romans pronounced a curse upon the site and forbade that the city should be rebuilt. But it was rebuilt. As the Phoenicians had come to Byrsa Hill, so other men from other lands came in the centuries that followed. Today, the city of Tunis stands a few miles from the site of ancient Carthage and the country of Tunisia occupies the central position on the North African coast which men so long found desirable.

Natural forces shaped Tunisia. From the beginning the sea was the highroad that led men to its shores. Its harbors on the east coast offered shelter to sailors, traders, and settlers. The position of the site made it a crossroads whose occupants in ancient times dominated the Mediterranean. The Sahara Desert at its back protected it against contacts from lands to the south.

Tunisia lies at the center of the Mediterranean Sea, only ninety miles from Sicily. Its neighbors on the north coast of Africa are Algeria and Libya. Tunisia is about the size of Louisiana.

Tunisia is largely a plateau, broken in the northern part of the country by several low mountain ranges. A coastal region in the north and east provides farming land. Southern Tunisia merges with the Sahara Desert. The Medjerda, Tunisia's only river of consequence, flows into the Gulf of Tunis.

The rainfall of Tunisia is one of the natural conditions that have shaped the development of the country. The best-watered part, a small area in the northwest, provides the source of the Medjerda River. The remainder of the northern and eastern sections receive from fifteen to twenty inches of rain per year, which falls during the winter months. In southern and western Tunisia the rainfall is very scanty.

The summers along the coast are hot and dry. The winters are cool and rainy. In the interior the summers are hotter than on the coast, the winters are colder and less rainy.

When Phoenicians came exploring the coast of North Africa they found there a fair-skinned people who came to be known as Berbers. They herded sheep and goats and raised grain and fruit. As people from the East claimed the better land, the Berbers retired to more remote areas, but they kept their own language and ways of living.

In spite of their curse upon the site, the Romans rebuilt Carthage and occupied it for four hundred years. Many Roman ruins still survive in Tunisia. After Roman power declined other groups of people, one after another, invaded the country. Vandals, Byzantines, Arabs, Spaniards, and Ottoman Turks each ruled for a time. The Arabs had the most lasting effect upon Tunisia, for they firmly established there the Arabic language and Islam, the religion of the followers of the Prophet Mohammed.

The Turks placed Tunisia under a ruler known as a bey who acknowledged the sultan of Turkey as his superior, but the sultan exercised little control over Tunisia. The beys contracted debts which they failed to settle. This led France in 1881 to establish a protectorate over Tunisia. By terms of the treaty which established the protectorate, the bey remained the ruler in name, but France exercised all real authority.

Under the protectorate a number of Frenchmen and Italians settled in Tunisia. Many of the Europeans secured holdings of the better land. Some of them engaged in business and industry. Europeans, especially Frenchmen, provided a large part of the professional men.

Early in this century some of the young men of Tunisia began to demand reforms which would secure greater rights and advantages for the Tunisians. They were later joined by older men and Tunisia's first political party was formed. The name of the party, *Destour*, is an Arabic word meaning Constitution. A few years later a young Tunisian, Habib Bourguiba, who was studying law in Paris, returned to Tunisia, and became involved in political activities. Seven years after his return from France Bourguiba became the leader of the Neo-Destour Party, which grew out of the earlier organization.

The French authorities resisted the demands of the Neo-Destour Party. Some of its leaders, including Bourguiba, were sent to prison, but the demand for reforms grew and developed into a movement for independence. Resistance to French rule involved some guerilla fighting by Tunisians as well as much negotiation. The resistance was climaxed on March 20, 1956, by French recognition of the independence of Tunisia. During the next year the Tunisians removed the bey and declared their nation a republic. A constitution was written and adopted. National elections were held in 1959, and Habib Bourguiba was elected the first President of Tunisia.

Bourguiba was re-elected in 1964 at the end of his first five-year term. Habib Bourguiba is not only the President of the Republic but also the head of his political party, recently renamed the Socialist Destourian Party. This is the only legal political party in Tunisia.

Under the French regime many western ways were introduced. Some of these persist and the French language is still widely used. Arabic is the basic language but it lacks the vocabulary for teaching modern science. There is no separation of church and state in the thinking of devout Moslems (followers of Islam), yet Tunisian leaders see values in the western idea that government and religion have separate functions. Islam required that women live much in seclusion and veil their faces when in public. Western thought holds that women should take a responsible part in affairs, free of such restrictions. In these and many other situations, Tunisians are caught in a conflict between eastern and western ideas and practices.

Agriculture is the basis of Tunisian economy and the source of many of its problems. Because of scarce rainfall much land cannot be used for farming. The land has been divided by inheritance until plots have often become too small to be operated profitably as individual farms. Under the French protectorate there were two systems of farming: a modern system operated by Europeans, who usually had the best land and good techniques, and a primitive system operated by Tunisians, who often had neither good land nor scientific methods. Another problem grew out of an ancient practice which permitted certain religious bodies to hold land in trust. Such land was untaxed, it often lay idle, and it could not pass into individual ownership. Tribal lands which were often not well used presented another problem.

The agricultural reforms undertaken by the government of independent Tunisia sought to solve existing problems. By irrigation and the use of the best-known methods of dry farming, more land was brought under cultivation and land already in use was made more profitable. Tiny plots were combined into larger units. Other measures were put into effect to take over lands owned by Europeans. Such land was expropriated, or taken by the Tunisian government without payment. There may be some later adjustment concerning payment, but only time will tell. The tracts held in trust by the religious bodies were also taken over and sold. The government negotiated with tribesmen in an effort to secure more effective use of tribal lands.

The most important plan put into effect was the establishment of co-operative farms sufficiently large to permit the use of modern equipment. On a co-operative farm a group of farmers work together under a trained farm manager. The co-operating farmers own equipment in common and share the profits of the enterprise. Each family is provided with a house and a small plot of land to be used as the family wishes. Such community services as a store, a school, a mosque, and a dispensary are usually available to the workers on a co-operative farm.

Agricultural products of Tunisia include livestock, small grains, olives, dates, grapes, figs, and other fruits. In the arid south, alfa grass, which grows wild, is harvested by seasonal agricultural workers and sold for the manufacture of cellulose products.

Phosphate, iron, lead, and zinc are produced in Tunisia. The principal manufactured products are olive oil, wine, soap, perfumes, fertilizer, carpets, blankets, shoes, and processed foods. There is extensive tunny and sponge fishing off Tunisian coasts.

Roads, bridges, airports, schoolhouses, and other types of construction were needed when independence came to Tunisia. An extensive public works program to meet these needs was established and is still underway. This program also helps provide employment for workers who would otherwise be unemployed.

In 1962 the government launched a ten-year economic development program. This program is assisted by foreign aid, about half of which comes from the United States.

One of the first measures that President Bourguiba sponsored was the abolishment of polygamy, a practice permitted to Moslems under their religious laws. This was a step toward raising the status of women. During the disturbed years before independence many children wandered the streets without homes or care. To meet their needs children's homes, known as Bourguiba Villages, were established. President Bourguiba has been deeply concerned with securing improvements in housing, schools, health services, labor laws, and other aspects of living.

In all reform measures the President has favored gradual progress, but he has kept up steady pressure for putting measures into action that would give Tunisians not only a better standard of living but better lives. More than any other leader, Bourguiba is the father of independent Tunisia.

Tunisia is a nation at the crossroads. It occupies the physical site which in ancient times was the crossroads for migrations of people. Today it is a crossroads where Arabic and western cultures meet. Standing at this juncture the Tunisian people feel the pull of both the East and the West and seek to integrate the patterns of life and thought of the two areas into a harmonious whole that is truly Tunisian culture.

We arrived in Tunis after a memorable flight over the Sahara Desert. We were assisted in setting up interviews by Mr. Richard Graham, Director of the Peace Corps in Tunisia, and the members of the Peace Corps staff. Certain members of the staff generously provided us transportation to distant points in their own cars.

Shaping a Nation Through Its People

When we arrived at the Pilot Study Center for Maternal and Child Health in Tunis, Peggy Gallen stood in the doorway of a small treatment room. Sterile syringes awaited her use. Fluid for injections was prepared. Peggy Gallen, Peace Corps nurse, was ready for her first patient of the day.

Peggy's special service was to inject fluid under the skin of babies suffering from diarrhea, an ailment that causes severe loss of body fluids. Before the injection treatment was begun at the Center many of the small patients afflicted with diarrhea died.

Peggy also prepared rice water and placed it in sterile bottles. The mothers used the rice water to feed the sick babies.

"In August when the weather was hot and diarrhea was at its worst, I often injected ten babies a day and handed out twenty-five bottles of rice water," Peggy reported to us. Then she added proudly, "Most of my babies lived. We had fewer deaths than ever before."

The mothers and babies whom Peggy served lived in areas in which sanitation was lacking. Many of the patients at the Pilot Center were Bedouin women and children whose families had been induced by the government to give up their usual tribal wandering and settle down in the community.

Looking out at the reception room of the Center, where 120 women and children waited, row by row on backless benches, Peggy commented, "They live without any conveniences, but they are surprisingly clean."

The appearance of the women bore out Peggy's statement. Most of them were dressed in the white sheetlike garment

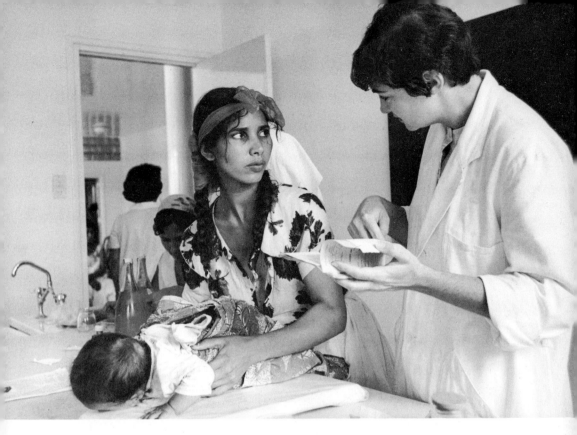

Peggy Gallen talks with an anxious mother about her sick baby.

called a *saffsari*, worn with one end held across the lower part of the face. As the women busied themselves with their babies some of them held their saffsaris with their teeth. The women wore brightly colored sweaters and jackets under their saffsaris and sandals or flat-heeled shoes on their feet. Many of the women were adorned with earrings and necklaces, but the most conspicuous adornments of the Bedouins were tattoo marks. The marks were dots arranged to form a pattern on forehead, cheeks, and chin, or in some cases on arms or legs.

With the arrival of four doctors who serviced the Center the place sprang into action. A nurse checked personal records. Another nurse passed up and down the benches taking the temperatures of the babies and issuing cards of admission to see a doctor or midwife. The women moved by turns into the various consulting rooms and from there went to the pharmacy for medicines or to treatment rooms, as they were directed to do.

A baby needing an injection of fluid was sent to Peggy's treatment room. The mother watched anxiously and the baby screamed heartily while Peggy shot sixteen ounces of fluid into the small body, four ounces in each shoulder, four more in each hip. In her best Arabic Peggy tried to assure the mother that the baby was improved by the treatment. In spite of Peggy's effort with the language, her words were not understood by the mother, but, reassured by the child's plump appearance, the mother rewarded Peggy with a glowing smile.

The Center was opened shortly after Tunisia won its independence as one answer to the demand for health services. The Center, which was equipped by UNICEF, is operated by the Tunisian government in co-operation with the World Health Organization, an agency of the United Nations. It is directed by Dr. Raouf Ben Brahem, a Tunisian, who is assisted by three doctors from other countries. A foreign nurse, the Peace Corps volunteer nurse, and several Tunisian nurses and midwives serve at the Center.

Because this is a Pilot Center, charts were designed and procedures developed and tried here. As these were found to be successful they were put to use in other maternal and child health centers which were opened across the country. The Pilot Center also provides several types of training for Tunisian health workers.

The Pilot Center provides prenatal care as well as care for babies and mothers. The Center sponsors classes where mothers are taught proper feeding and bathing of infants. Because the women have lived in primitive conditions they sometimes need instructions about very elementary matters. Some of the women have to be shown how to turn on a water spigot. Others have to learn how to sit on a bench.

Peggy Gallen, in the second year of her Peace Corps experience in Tunisia, found her work at the Pilot Center for Maternal and Child Health more rewarding than her first year's experience in the maternity ward at a city hospital. After Peggy was transferred to the Pilot Center, where she could count accomplishment in terms of babies saved, she said, "If I had it to do over, even knowing all I know now, I'd join the Peace Corps."

Peggy meant what she said. After completing her service as a volunteer, she enlisted as a staff nurse and is serving in this capacity with the Peace Corps staff doctor in Guinea.

Peggy was an experienced obstetrical nurse before she became a volunteer, but she was frustrated in the Tunisian hospital. Her sense of frustration was shared by many of the other twenty-two Peace Corps nurses then serving in Tunisian hospitals. The unsatisfactory situation had several causes. Nursing does not command the respect in Tunisia that it does in America. The Tunisian government asked for nurses to give expert patient care. It was thought that the work of Peace Corps nurses might develop pride in nursing and commitment to it. While there was no agreement before the nurses arrived that they would teach nursing, the Peace Corps emphasizes to all volunteers their responsibility for teaching their counterparts new skills and techniques. In Tunisia the Peace Corps nurses found little opportunity to do this. Tunisian nurses, trained in the French system of nursing, felt no need for learning new techniques, and furthermore they had little confidence in American medical and nursing practices because they considered the American system of medicine inferior to the French system that they had learned.

The problems between the Tunisian and American nurses were increased by poor communication. Today all volunteers going to Tunisia have excellent training in French and Arabic, but the first volunteers had no training in Arabic and were not always fluent in French. The Tunisians usually spoke no English. The many differences created dissatisfaction among Peace Corps nurses serving in Tunisian hospitals, although about one third of the first group of nurses, before they completed their tour of duty, were given responsibility for the in-service training of student nurses.

In the school year beginning in 1963 there were four Peace Corps volunteers teaching in Tunisia. A year later there were seventy volunteers teaching in the country. That year the Tunisian Peace Corps director stated that the purpose of the Corps was to expand the teaching program still further. The growth of teaching as a Peace Corps activity had its basic cause in the need for teachers, created by the eagerness of young Tunisians to secure education and the efforts of the government to provide educational opportunities.

The increased use of volunteers to meet this need was made possible when school administrators were persuaded that volunteers were competent to teach. In the beginning, even with an acute shortage of teachers, some men in the Ministry of Education resisted using volunteers because they believed that only French-trained teachers were competent. When the first volunteers succeeded, these men relaxed their resistance and agreed to try using more volunteers in Tunisian schools. Educational authorities have learned to value volunteer teachers not only because of their competence in their subject matter but also because of their enthusiasm and dedication.

Language training is important in Tunisian secondary schools and colleges. Students learn Arabic and usually French and one other modern language as well. The trend now is for students to choose English as the second modern language. Many of the Peace Corps volunteers taught English, sometimes with another subject, but often as a full program.

The volunteers served in a variety of schools. Many taught at the secondary level, some in academic and some in vocational schools. Several volunteers taught in colleges, nine were at the Bourguiba Institute of Living Languages, and a few were at the aviation school conducted by the International Civil Aeronautics Organization of the United Nations (ICAO).

English has been adopted as the international language of aviation. All personnel concerned with international flights are required to have a command of English. Schools to train such personnel have been established at various points throughout the world by the ICAO. The aviation school for Africa is located at the international airport that serves Tunis. Peace Corps volunteers taught English in that school.

George Talbot, volunteer in Tunisia, teaches an English class.

The Bourguiba Institute of Living Languages was founded in 1956 by the United States Information Service. Its purpose was to give rapid training in English to adults whose work required immediate facility in the language. Among its first students were Tunisian policemen who were to be sent to the United States for training in police work. The Institute undertook to give them in a short time a reasonable command of English.

The USIS operated the program until 1960, when the Institute and the building in which it operated were turned over to the Tunisian government. The Institute was then made a part of the University of Tunis and its program was expanded to include other modern languages. The United States supplied teachers directly to the Institute until 1964 when it was decided to have the Peace Corps assign volunteers for the work. That year nine volunteers took over all the English instruction at the Institute. There were about five hundred students enrolled in the English classes.

Intensive courses were given in four-hour periods to persons who needed to gain quick command of the language. Among these persons were many who had won scholarships for study in the United States. The Institute offered other courses in English for persons able to learn a new language under more leisurely conditions. The Institute had become the major establishment for adult education in Tunisia.

Sharon Benge, a volunteer teaching one of the intensive courses at Bourguiba Institute, tossed questions at the young men seated before her. They answered rapidly, at first in chorus, then one by one.

"What day of the week is today?" Sharon asked.

"Today is Thursday," the class answered.

"What is the plural of 'box'?" Sharon continued.

"The plural of 'box' is 'boxes,'" the class proclaimed.

When the individual drill began the answers were crisp and clear as the students replied in full sentences to Sharon's questions.

The oral English drill continued for several minutes, to the obvious pleasure of the students, who enjoyed practicing their spoken English. Then Sharon changed the pace by introducing a young man to his neighbor. When the neighbor had properly acknowledged the introduction, he in turn performed an introduction. The chain of introductions and acknowledgments continued around the class until each member had had practice in performing in English a necessary social courtesy.

Interest was high and the desire of the students to master the language was evident. Sharon, and the co-teacher who served with her in the four-hour period, provided a wide variety of drill, both oral and written, all designed to help the students gain a basic knowledge of English.

Neglected children! Lonely children! Homeless children! Hungry children! Beggar children! Delinquent children! Tunisia had them all! In July 1956, three months after independence, a Children's Village was opened to shelter 760 of the homeless boys and girls. Other villages were soon established, some to care for boys, some for girls.

Kurt Liske believes that Bourguiba Villages and the Peace Corps have much to give each other. Kurt should know, for he is serving his third year in a Bourguiba Village. After his first tour of duty ended Kurt went home for a vacation. He spent part of it serving as assistant director in a boys' summer camp. But his heart was still in the Children's Village program in Tunisia. He re-enlisted in the Peace Corps and returned to work in the Bourguiba Villages.

The Villages were established to care for orphans, but the program was later expanded to include children from families unable to give their children adequate care and education. Among the children entering the Villages under this provision were young Bedouins whose parents had difficulties finding work under Tunisia's Bedouin resettlement program.

Younger Village children attend primary school, usually in

the local community. Those who have finished primary school are given vocational training, though a boy or girl with marked academic ability may instead receive instruction at an academic secondary school. Children entering the Villages are tested and placed in locations suited to their abilities. A young person stays in his Village until he has completed training and has been placed in a job.

Kurt Liske's first assignment as a Peace Corps volunteer was to the Bourguiba Village at Zaghouan. The Village is perched high on a hill above the town in an old French army camp. The buildings had been adapted for their new purpose and some new buildings erected. The Village, administered by a director and an assistant director, was for older boys, and its program was primarily for training in carpentry, masonry, and machine-shop work. The two hundred boys at the Zaghouan Village lived in six dormitories, each headed by a monitor. Kurt and other staff members were comfortably housed. There was a gymnasium and a small library.

In addition to all of these pleasant circumstances, Kurt, a history major, found to his delight that Zaghouan was in the midst of Roman ruins. He inspected the aqueducts that had once carried water to Tunis and visited the temple built by the Romans at the source of the waters. The young volunteer was pleased with his location. Zaghouan seemed a promising Village in which to work.

Kurt's assignment was to teach physical education. Another volunteer in the Village had the same assignment. The two young men reported to the gymnasium, eager to start classes. There they suffered their first setback, for they soon discovered that the Village was well staffed by Tunisians. There was little for the volunteers to do. In this program, as in the teaching of English, some authorities had little confidence in the ability of Peace Corps volunteers. Even though the Tunisian government had requested volunteers, certain men in authority did not at first make a place for them on the Village staffs.

Looking back at this experience, Kurt later said, "For several months I did only four hours a week of real work. I was surely frustrated."

The frustration that the two volunteers felt drove them to action. All the physical education taught in the Village had been formal gymnastics. There had never been a competitive sports program. Kurt and his partner started one. They organized and coached dormitory teams and soon had a flourishing intramural program going with competition in handball, volleyball, chess, and ping-pong.

The boys responded to the new program, their first organized recreation, with joyous enthusiasm. Encouraged by the boys' response, the volunteers introduced basketball at Zaghouan. Basketball was played in Tunisia but it was not a highly developed sport there. It had received a boost, however, shortly before the volunteers introduced the game at Zaghouan. During the Christmas vacation Peace Corps volunteers working in physical education organized themselves into teams and went on a tour playing exhibition games. The tour stimulated increased interest in the game.

A new spirit began to emerge at Zaghouan. The boys displayed pride in the achievements of their dormitory teams. When Village basketball teams were organized Village spirit grew stronger.

The Bourguiba Children's Villages are under the direction of a government agency called the Department of Youth and Sport. Near the end of Kurt's first year in Tunisia, the volunteers working in physical education and sports had a conference with representatives of the Department. The Tunisians approved sports programs such as Kurt and his partner had developed at Zaghouan. Recalling the Tunisians' change in attitude toward volunteers, Kurt later said, "They had to be convinced by experience that Peace Corps volunteers could do what needed to be done."

Kurt was aware that volunteers in other fields of work in

Tunisia had encountered a similar lack of confidence on the part of Tunisian authorities. Kurt offered what he believed was the explanation of this attitude, when he said, "Because Peace Corps volunteers came over here and worked for little or no money, the Tunisians thought they must be either crazy or inefficient."

After work in a summer camp for boys, Kurt was sent for his second year's service to the Bourguiba Village at Haffouz. At this village older boys were trained to carry on agricultural work with power equipment. Kurt had a Tunisian counterpart at Haffouz, a young man who was competent in sports. Kurt taught physical education, coached the basketball team and the cross-country runners, and co-operated with his counterpart on track and field sports. During the Christmas vacation Kurt and other volunteers working in sports held a basketball clinic for boys from the Bourguiba Villages. Kurt counted his months at Haffouz as well spent. He gained valuable experience and the Village sports program flourished.

For his third year Kurt was sent back to Zaghouan. He was the only volunteer in the Village at the time, but he had a Tunisian counterpart who also became his good friend. Kurt taught physical education, ran an intramural sports program, and coached the Village junior and senior basketball teams. Kurt lived with a Tunisian teacher in a small apartment at the Village but he ate his lunch and dinner with his counterpart's family in the town. The counterpart's mother had formerly been a cook at the palace of the Bey of Tunisia, so Kurt became well acquainted with Tunisian delicacies. His daily visits to his friend's home also provided practice in speaking Arabic and an opportunity to become familiar with Arabic culture. In his third year in Tunisia Kurt Liske found life at Zaghouan good.

Shaping a Nation Through Physical Changes

On the flat roof of a partially completed schoolhouse in Tunisia a half dozen men lounged, enjoying the evening coolness that had wiped out the daytime heat. The remains of the supper they had just finished were scattered about—one lamb chop left on a pan, a few olives, the crusty end of a loaf of French bread, and a half-empty wine bottle.

The men were young. All but one were Tunisians. The tall, blond chap was an American—the only American in Souk el Arba.

The men in the little group on the roof were friends and fellow workers in the building of the schoolhouse. Talk flowed easily among them as they relaxed on the roof. But the talk was not of their daily tasks. These were young men with the curious minds and the wide-ranging interests of youth. The presence of the American was an added stimulus to talk of far places and unfamiliar ways of life. So the Tunisians put question after question to their American friend.

They asked about the American's homeland—about its vast size and about its wealth that enabled even workingmen to drive automobiles. They asked, with a trifle of embarrassment, how it felt to take a girl on that strange something that Americans called "a date." But their most eager questions concerned politics. They wanted to know if Americans were free to vote as they wished—or not to vote at all. They wondered if the often-mentioned American democracy was real. They asked if the American principle of equality was actually practiced.

Lowell Sykes, the American, had questions, too. After many months in Tunisia he was still trying to understand its people, to find what it was that made them think and act in their own particular way. So his questions sought to discover the power that religion and patriotism gave to their lives. And he wondered why so many Tunisians followed the old ways instead of experimenting with new ways, as Americans do.

The exchange of ideas and opinions flowed back and forth. And when at long last the evening was done every man in the group had grown in understanding and had deepened his sense of fellowship with the other men.

Lowell Sykes was one of eleven Peace Corps volunteers who went to Tunisia to supervise construction at the beginning of the Peace Corps program in that country. The men were trained to work with block and rubble construction, commonly used in village housing. When the volunteers arrived they found that the Tunisians wanted construction foremen trained to supervise work on high-rise, reinforced concrete, and steel structures. None of the eleven was prepared to do this type of supervision.

The lack of clear understanding between the Peace Corps and the Tunisian Ministry of Public Works caused frustration for the volunteers involved. The problems were increased by the volunteers' difficulties with language. They were not yet fluent in French and they had had no instruction in Arabic. Laborers often spoke only Arabic.

The eleven volunteers were sent to various towns and assigned to reinforced concrete construction, where they could do little except observe. After five months the volunteers were called back to Tunis. The Tunisian Ministry of Public Works and American authorities planned a pilot project to show what could be done with simple housing. The plan called for building four cinder-block houses, each with one room and a detached kitchen and toilet. Tunisian workmen were to build two of the houses, the Peace Corps volunteers the other two.

The volunteers were delighted with the opportunity to dem-

onstrate their skills and fell to work with a will. It was soon
evident, however, that the Tunisians had no intention of per-
mitting the Americans to build their two houses unaided and
undirected. Apparently without any sense of embarrassment,
the Tunisians swarmed over the houses on which the volunteers
were working. They criticized and offered suggestions endlessly.
If a volunteer carried a board up a ladder, a Tunisian carried
it down again. Recalling this phase of his experience Lowell
said, "It was like the Keystone Kops."

After two weeks the four houses were done and the eleven
volunteers were again unemployed. By this time three of them
had had enough. They resigned from the Peace Corps and
returned home.

Lowell and the others remained, still hoping to find real work
to do. After a time Lowell heard of a need in a Bourguiba Village and was sent there. A large building that could be converted into a gymnasium had in the center two huge concrete
blocks. How to get the blocks removed was the problem. Lowell
enlisted the aid of an American construction company that was
building an airstrip near by. The company lent an air com-
pressor and jackhammer and the services of a mechanic. In four
days the blocks were out. Lowell supervised the reconstruction
of the building. Two months later the Village had a beautiful
gymnasium and Lowell was once more unemployed.

After two months of errand-running at the Peace Corps
office, Lowell was assigned to teach sheet-metal work in an
apprentice school run by the International Labor Organization
of the United Nations. Lowell's spirits rose, for this was work
that he knew how to do. But the director of the school, a
Frenchman, declared that Lowell did not know enough French
to teach. For six months Lowell set up equipment, listened to
another man teach the class, and grew ever more discouraged.
But he continued to practice his French and he took up the
study of classical Arabic.

Lowell contracted infectious hepatitis and spent a month in

the hospital and two months more recuperating in his apartment. He had a great deal of time to think and to evaluate his Peace Corps service. Though his two-year tour of duty was nearing an end, Lowell decided that he still wanted a job in which he could prove his ability and render useful service. As Lowell put it, "I wanted to build my Peace Corps image the way I thought it should be."

The Peace Corps received a call for a man to supervise the construction of a schoolhouse in Souk el Arba. Lowell was offered the job. He could have gone home at the end of his tour of duty, but he was not willing to quit short of accomplishment so he asked for an extension and set out for Souk el Arba.

Lowell had no problem about living a simple life in Souk el Arba. There was little housing. He found an empty tool room in a new school for apprentices, secured permission to live there, and moved in. His furniture consisted of a cot, a chair, and his two suitcases. But the school had showers and a toilet, which he used, and a watchman from whom he learned much Arabic. The tool room was his home for seven months.

On this job Lowell was given real authority. As he put the matter, "By this time I had learned enough to be effective. I had learned French and Arabic, Tunisian methods of building, and the Tunisian mentality."

Lowell's fellow workers on the construction job were cooperative and pleasant. Some of them became his staunch friends, with whom he often shared suppers and long talks during his months in Souk el Arba.

At the end of his Peace Corps service Lowell Sykes had the satisfaction of knowing that he had not quit. He had helped in the construction of a school building. And he had forged bonds of brotherhood with men of another culture.

After Tunisia became independent, architects were in short supply. Before independence nearly all the architects were

Don Watson visits the housing project he planned in Sfax, Tunisia.

Frenchmen. Most of these men withdrew from Tunisia after the country became independent. The shortage was doubly serious because Tunisia needed to launch a public works program. When Peace Corps service became available the Tunisian government promptly requested volunteer architects.

In the fall of 1962 twelve young men arrived in Tunisia in answer to the call. Eleven of them were architects, one was a specialist in city planning. All had had university training in their chosen fields but none had had much experience.

Tunisian government officials needed experienced architects. They accepted the volunteers and assigned them to duty under the Ministry of Public Works, but they gave many of them what the young architects considered "busy work." Only a few of the volunteers were put on real projects. Since Tunisia had

limited funds it was reasonable to put the architects through a
trial period, but the young men were impatient at what they
felt was unnecessary delay. But in time the Ministry began to
give the architects responsible assignments.

Once over its first difficulties, the architectural program
moved forward well in Tunisia. After the Peace Corps and the
American Institute of Architects signed a contract, Mr. Na-
thaniel Firestone went to Tunisia, in 1964, to become the
Contractor's Overseas Representative. His function was to provide professional support to the volunteers working in architecture, engineering, and city planning. The projects were assigned
by the Ministry but Mr. Firestone gave continuous supervision
to the volunteers in these fields.

By late 1964 there were forty-six men carrying out assignments made by the Ministry of Public Works. These assignments reflected the plans of the government to improve Tunisia
through physical changes. Volunteers planned schoolhouses,
city halls, markets, dormitories, social centers, and other buildings for community use. They designed and landscaped housing
projects in the towns. They helped plan housing, roads, and
other services in the new farm communities which the government is establishing as it settles the nomadic tribes in permanent locations.

Certain volunteers, under Mr. Firestone's supervision, aided
the nation's archaeologists in their efforts to preserve relics of
historical value. Since field work among the ruins can be done
only during the dry season the young men helping in this area
did architectural planning in the rainy season.

Sfax, one of Tunisia's leading cities, has been the center of
much public improvement. Don Watson arrived with the first
volunteer architects and was assigned to Sfax. Twenty-four
months later he was still there. He had then extended for four
months and had so many projects still underway that the date
when he would terminate his service was not yet decided.

After a trial period at the beginning of his service in Tunisia

Don was assigned to plan a dormitory for a secondary school at Monastir. He was given two weeks in which to make preliminary plans. It seemed an impossible deadline, but Don knew he must meet it, for this was a project in which President Bourguiba was deeply interested and the President was coming to Monastir to see the plans.

Don went into a frenzy of activity. On the appointed day he had ready a model of the building and a memorized speech of explanation. He never had an opportunity to deliver that speech, because President Bourguiba asked questions so fast that Don was kept busy answering him. Don was impressed by the President's knowledge of architecture and vastly relieved when the President approved his model and he was told to execute drawings.

Before Don had these drawings completed he was involved in projects in and near Sfax, and from that time on he had a heavy schedule. In his first twenty-four months he worked on twenty-four projects. At the end of that period twelve of the twenty-four buildings were completed, six were nearing completion, and the other six were in various stages of waiting. Don's duties included both drawing plans and supervising construction. He found that working days could be stretched to twelve or fourteen hours and that a healthy young American could go two years without a vacation, even though he is entitled to one month's leave each year.

One of Don's plans for a primary school proved so satisfactory that forty such schools were erected. The building, constructed of fieldstone and provided with improved lighting, had the added virtue of economical cost.

Don experimented with several original ideas for securing proper light without glare, but he sometimes had to overcome the objection that his idea could not be followed because such an idea had never been used in Tunisia. In one case so simple a change as painting a concrete overhang gray to reduce glare met objection because this had never been done.

Don planned to continue in service until the six unfinished buildings were completed. He then hoped to prepare, with help from the other Peace Corps architects, a technical handbook on Tunisian building methods, materials, and practices. Don felt that he had gained valuable experience and made some contribution to the public works program in Tunisia. Through the handbook he hoped to aid both Tunisian technicians and Peace Corps architects to make even greater contributions in the future.

Tunisia is engaged in a huge road-building program in which many machines are used. As soon as Peace Corps service became available, officials of the Tunisian government requested mechanics to keep the heavy road-building equipment in repair.

John Martinkovich was in the first group of mechanics that went to Tunisia in answer to the government's request. He had worked twelve years as a mechanic before he joined the Peace Corps.

John discovered a great difference in attitude between the Tunisians and Americans concerning the maintenance of equipment. The prime purpose of the Tunisians was to push construction as rapidly as possible. A large number of miles constructed in a short period of time became a mark of status. To attain this end the Tunisians used machinery without letup until it broke down. American mechanics had been taught to practice preventive maintenance. Under this plan a machine was taken out of use at regular intervals for inspection and minor repairs.

John and the other mechanics struggled with this difference in point of view throughout their service in Tunisia without any general conversion of Tunisian road builders. But here and there the mechanics did convince some individuals that in the end more miles of road could be built when machinery was kept in repair than when it was pushed to a complete breakdown.

John was sometimes depressed by hampering conditions that he could not overcome, but his usually buoyant nature always asserted itself. At the end of an extended tour of duty, John Martinkovich said, "I feel some satisfaction with my work." John had an additional reward, for romance blossomed for him in Tunisia. He and one of the Peace Corps volunteer nurses, nearing the end of her tour of duty, were planning their wedding, scheduled to take place shortly after their return to America.

The improvement of farming is an important part of Tunisia's development program. The Tunisian government secured the co-operation of the Food and Agricultural Organization of the United Nations in this program of improvement. Among other services rendered, the FAO operated experimental farms in Tunisia. The terms of the experiment called for FAO opera-

John Martinkovich explains equipment maintenance to a mechanic.

tion for five years, after which the farms were to be turned over to the Tunisian government. Peace Corps volunteers served on two of the farms in Central Tunisia while these were under the direction of FAO.

The FAO farm, Center of Ousseltia, was located on land formerly owned by French farmers. Local Tunisians were employed on the farm, which comprised about four thousand acres. An experienced and competent agricultural specialist from Italy managed the farm for FAO, with the help of an able Tunisian assistant.

The volunteers who worked at the Center of Ousseltia were Fred Sanz and his wife Sandra, a nurse, Kenneth Knoll, and Gayle Norris. The farm used a good deal of power equipment and Fred and Ken had responsibility for its maintenance. Gayle's assignment was to work with pasture management and forage crops. All three of the men had Tunisian counterparts. Gayle also had an FAO man working with him in a counterpart relationship. The volunteers thought that some of the counterparts gained considerable knowledge about better farming practices.

The Center of Ousseltia lay in an area where the average rainfall was only twelve or thirteen inches per year. There was no irrigation so the best dry-farming methods were used. Such methods included careful preparation of the seedbed, the elimination of all weeds, and cultivation of row-planted crops. The purpose of dry-farming practices is to conserve moisture.

On this farm the new agricultural practices, developed experimentally, included the selection of seeds for the purpose of finding varieties adapted to the prevailing natural conditions, the proper use of commercial fertilizers, contour plowing and other types of soil conservation, and various aspects of farm management.

Sandra Sanz worked in a government dispensary that provided out-patient care for the people in the community. A doctor visited the dispensary two days each week. He wrote out orders, which Sandra and the three Tunisian nurses at the dispensary carried out.

The FAO farm, Center of Ouled Mohamed, was located on land belonging to a tribe of Bedouins. The government made a contract with the tribe to secure the use of about four thousand acres of their tribal holdings for a farm, and to employ the men of the tribe on the farm. The government then asked FAO to establish an experimental farm on the land.

Many of the Bedouins lived in a village on the farm. Others lived in tents and houses on tribal lands outside the farm area.

A well fifteen hundred feet deep was drilled. This insured a water supply for the farm and for the Bedouins. Water was piped to their village. Those who lived farther away carried it to their homes in jars and kegs on the backs of donkeys. Nothing could have done as much to secure for the experiment the good will of the Bedouins as the production of abundant water.

The water was sufficient to irrigate one hundred acres of the land. On the remainder of the cultivated land dry-farming methods were employed. Some of the acreage was used for grazing sheep and cattle.

The volunteers serving in agriculture at Center of Ouled Mohamed were Stewart McKenzie and Dick Hinson. At the end of his first year on the farm, Stewart McKenzie married one of the Peace Corps nurses stationed in Tunis and took her to live at the farm. The Peace Corps assigned Connie McKenzie some responsibility for health services to the Bedouins living nearby.

Stew McKenzie helped in the operation of the FAO farm's irrigation system. He also worked with crop production. Stew had a Tunisian counterpart with a receptive attitude toward learning, who was a graduate of an agricultural secondary school. Dick Hinson, a Missouri farm boy with a taste for power machinery, worked as a farm mechanic. He too had a counterpart.

A program to teach proper feeding and care of livestock enabled the Bedouins who owned sheep and cattle to realize greater profits on their animals. Under the program a Bedouin owner paid to the farm a small fee for each animal that received care. For sheep the farm provided flock management, spraying to destroy parasites, and the use of grazing grounds. For cattle the farm established a feeding program that included the use of silage, forage crops, and hay. The Bedouins were pleased with the increased yields of wool and milk. They were even more pleased when they discovered the profits to be made by purchasing skinny cattle from other tribesmen, fattening them under the feeding program, and selling them.

The demonstration of the value of feeding and management programs for livestock was one of the substantial accomplishments of the experimental farm at Center of Ouled Mohamed. Other achievements, similar to those on the farm at Center of Ousseltia, demonstrated the profits to be gained from the use of good seed, fertilizers, soil conservation, certain new crops, and proper management.

The volunteers on both the FAO farms recognized these achievements but they had some doubts about the ability of the Tunisians to make full use, after the withdrawal of FAO personnel, of methods so far in advance of those to which the farmers had long been accustomed. The volunteers pointed out that Tunisians are handicapped in agriculture, as in other areas of living, by extreme traditionalism, which tends to keep them following old patterns of thought and practice. On the other hand, as the volunteers recognized, there were signs here and there that a spark of interest in new ways had been kindled. In Tunisia, as elsewhere, such kindling of the spark is vital to the success of the Peace Corps program.

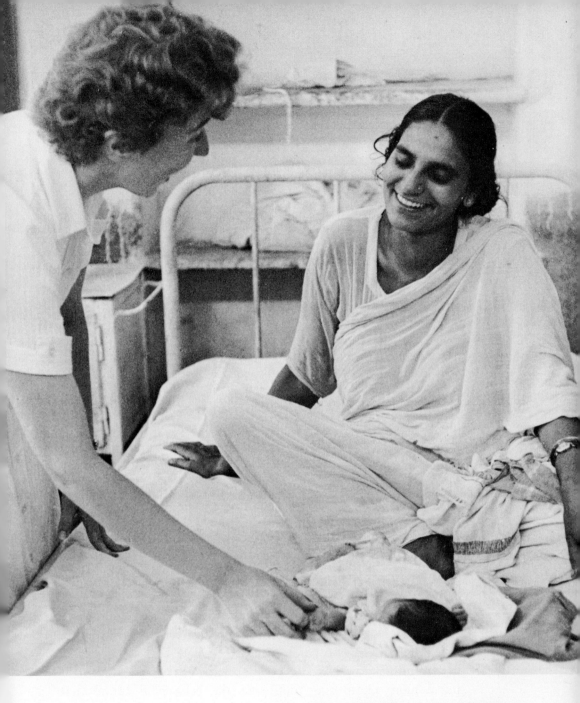

5. AT WORK IN INDIA

Old Land, New Republic

People, people everywhere!

India is a land pulsing with life. On the streets and roads, in public buildings, in the fields, everywhere we went there were people. Driving through the wide, tree-lined streets of New Delhi, the capital, we saw people on the move. Thousands rode bicycles, some rode back to back in horse-drawn carts, some lumbered over the pavement in two-wheeled bullock carts, or four-wheeled wagons, others jolted along in ancient taxicabs or traveled in the new-style three-wheeled taxis. Many rode in buses, a few drove automobiles, a great number walked.

In Old Delhi we saw all of these travelers and much more. On the sidewalks merchants sold their wares, artisans plied their trades, men squatted in conversation or slept in exhaustion, while constant streams of people on foot picked their way among the obstructions. And always there were the cows, for in India the cow is held in veneration by the Hindus, the most numerous religious group in the country. The cows wandered unmolested through the streets, helped themselves to bites at the vegetable stands, and nibbled at other promising prospects.

An automobile trip through the country in North India became an adventure in steering, as the driver leaned on his horn and slowly wove his way in and out of traffic. Here again were the carts, the wagons, the buses, and the occasional automobile. There were also trucks, herds of cattle and goats, and a never-ending procession of people, many carrying loads. Adding a more picturesque note was the occasional camel that stalked along drawing a cart, often with the driver stretched out on top of his load sound asleep. There was also the bicycle rickshaw that rolled along at a good clip, propelled by the pedaling rickshaw man.

On the map, India has the appearance of a giant triangle extending south from central Asia. Across its northern border stretch the Himalayas, the world's highest mountains. At the foot of the mountains a great plain fifteen hundred miles from east to west stretches across India and extends into Pakistan. Three river systems, the Indus, Ganges, and Brahmaputra, water the plain, which is divided into the three natural regions formed by the river systems. In the center of the triangular peninsula, the Deccan Plateau rises from one to two thousand feet high. The plateau is flanked to the east and west and separated from the northern plains by mountain chains. Around the coast of the triangle runs a fertile coastal plain.

India has three rather distinct seasons. Temperatures vary from south to north, but it is cold only in the mountainous region of the far north. Rainfall varies from heavy in the east to scanty in the west.

Religion has long been an important factor in India. Hinduism is the dominant religion, but it is much more than a religion, for it is also a way of life that provides for its followers a system with exact rules for every act of living. As part of its way of life, Hinduism has a caste system, developed from four classes of people, or orders of life, as set out in early Hindu writings. The four original castes were the priests, warriors, merchants, and farmers. These four castes have been divided and subdivided until there are now some three thousand castes.

Outside of the four orders were the outcastes, who were expected to do work, such as sweeping, considered unsuitable for caste Hindus. The outcastes were sometimes called the Untouchables because it was believed that a caste Hindu was polluted by touching an outcaste.

The Moslems form the second largest religious group in India. There are also people of other religious faiths, including

Christians, Jews, Buddhists, and certain reform Hindu groups such as the Jains and the Sikhs.

Civilization developed in India before history was written. Literature handed down by word of mouth for centuries before it was put in writing provides a picture of Indian life at the time and forms a core of religious writing that is held sacred by the Hindus.

The centuries after history was written were marked by the invasion of conquering armies and the rise and fall of ruling families. There were, however, some periods during these centuries when civilization flourished. One such period was the reign of the Emperor Ashoka, who ruled from 273 to 232 B.C. In the early years of his reign he extended his empire by bloody wars, but after he was converted to Buddhism he sought to promote peace and right living in the empire. He had his laws hewn on stone and placed before his people.

Another period of stable rule was achieved during the Gupta Dynasty, A.D. 320 to 647. Under the Guptas civilization flowered. Sanskrit, the sacred language of the Hindus, took form. Literature flourished. Sculptors produced notable work. Colleges attracted students. Indian mathematicians invented the numerals that we now use and developed the concept of zero and the decimal system.

The conquest by Moslems of a part of India in A.D. 1193 established the beginning of five hundred years of Moslem rule. The faith of the Moslems was in sharp conflict with the faith of the Hindus. Thus there began religious differences that were to continue and have a profound effect upon the later history of India.

Passing years brought other men to India. Some came as invaders, some came to trade. In 1600 the East India Company, an English trading venture, was chartered. The Company set up trading posts in India. Over the years British power increased until British rule was firmly established in India.

When the British began to assert their power they found some six hundred Indian princes each ruling a kingdom. Instead of displacing the princes, Britain made treaties with them. Their kingdoms were recognized as dependent states subject to the over-all authority of Britain, but with the ruling princes nominally in charge.

Britain made India a part of the British Empire in 1858. India continued in this relationship until 1947, when Britain granted independence and the Republic of India was established. As the demands for independence mounted in India, the differences between the Hindus and Moslems increased, marked by mutual suspicion and bloody riots. Finally it was agreed that two independent nations, India and Pakistan, should be established. Pakistan, to be a Moslem state, was made up of two parts, East and West Pakistan. Between the two stretched a thousand miles of Indian territory.

The early days of independence were marred by frightful massacres and by migrations of religious refugees between Pakistan and India. Eventually order was restored, though the enmity created by long differences, climaxed by violence, lingered to color Indian and Pakistani relations.

Mohandas Gandhi was a leader in India's drive for independence. He proposed a policy of non-co-operation with the British government and of passive resistance. These policies were helpful in the struggle for independence, but they often caused Gandhi to be sent to prison. Gandhi had political wisdom which he used to prepare younger men for the responsibility of self-government when it came. His choice for India's leader was Jawaharlal Nehru, who became independent India's first Prime Minister.

Nehru, the son of a wealthy father, was sent to Britain for his education. The training he received there in western political principles proved of great value as he led India into modern nationhood. The Indian way of peaceful change, impressed upon him by Gandhi, proved equally useful. India came to independence at a time of world crisis. It faced gigantic internal problems. Nehru led the young republic through the maze of difficulties that beset it.

India is a federal republic consisting of fourteen states and several territories. The Prime Minister is the head of the government.

India is a land of many tongues. There are fourteen officially recognized languages and over five hundred dialects. Friction developed over a requirement that Hindi should become the official national language. Citizens of India who are not Hindi-speaking people object to Hindi as the national language. English is sometimes used in India as a matter of convenience. It is generally used as the language of instruction in colleges and universities.

The government of newly independent India faced tremendous problems. The country had a huge population. The great majority of the people were desperately poor. Millions were hungry. Malnutrition, lack of sanitation, and disease combined to make a high death rate. Vast numbers of people could not read or write and lacked schools in which to learn. Many people were unable to find work. In some larger cities housing was so scarce that people lived and died on the streets.

Jawaharlal Nehru and his co-workers in government had courage and coupled with it they had a devotion to democratic processes. They made long-range plans by means of which they expected to overcome their difficulties. The first of a series of five-year plans was put into effect in 1951. India is now working under the Third Five-Year Plan, begun in 1961. If all goes as expected, two further five-year plans will follow to complete the long-range cycle projected soon after independence. Stated in general terms, the goals set in the planning aimed to improve agriculture in order to relieve the food shortage, to develop both large and small industry in order to provide employment and needed goods, and to improve living conditions through social services that aided health and education.

The government created a structure through which planning could be administered. Each state was divided into districts, each district into blocks. Each block had a staff headed by a block officer, who was assisted by persons concerned with the various aspects of the program, such as agriculture, animal husbandry, education, health, and industry.

Each block in rural India includes a number of villages. In order to involve the local people more fully in the planning process and to make the people more active participants in government, the activity of the village council, known as a *panchayat,* has been revived. The panchayat was an ancient institution that had fallen somewhat into disuse.

Certain conspicuous reforms authorized by law should be mentioned. Under the terms of India's constitution the caste system is not recognized, certain rights are guaranteed to the outcastes, and discrimination against them is punishable by law. The law has established the legal rights of women for the first time in the history of India. A considerable redistribution of land has been made under the terms of land reform acts.

India has made progress in overcoming its gigantic problems. The national income has increased, agricultural production has improved, industrial production has doubled, the number of students in school has increased from twenty-six to forty-six million, with girls and women now receiving education, which they rarely did in earlier years. Health services have been made available to most of the people. Heavy industries, notably steel mills, have been built. Outcastes are slowly gaining a better position in Indian life. Modern conditions, which make the observation of caste restrictions difficult, are helping to break down the caste system.

The improvements in internal conditions have been made at the same time that certain external problems had to be met.

India and Pakistan still have in dispute the final disposition of Kashmir, one of the former princely states. Red China still stands as a threat on India's northern border, where the Chinese have occupied land claimed by India.

The improvements achieved deserve high praise. The problems ahead are still staggering. Progress in India has been greatly helped by foreign aid, totaling about one billion dollars a year. The United States has furnished more than 40 per cent of the foreign aid received by India. If India is to continue to function as a free nation operating under constitutional government and democratic processes, internal improvement must go forward. Such improvement can be made only with the help of foreign aid. The Peace Corps is one element, though the smallest, in American aid to India.

We were guided in planning our schedule in India by Mr. Brent K. Ashabranner, then Deputy Director, and now Director of the Peace Corps in India. Mr. Ashabranner, like Dr. C. S. Houston, whom he succeeded, is determined that the Peace Corps shall help to tip the scales toward progress and freedom at this point in the history of India. As we drove about in hired cars, observing conditions at close range and discussing them with Indians and volunteers, we became keenly aware of the critical nature of India's problems.

Chickens and More Chickens

Four young men arrived at Nabha in Punjab State in December 1961. They were members of the first group of Peace Corps volunteers sent to India. Each had an assignment. Ken Sherper went into teaching and Tom Kessinger began to establish youth clubs. Sean Doherty, assigned to advise small industries, and Bill Donovan, sent to work in dairy extension, were unable to find work in their assigned fields. Week after week they cast around looking for suitable jobs, but it seemed that no one wanted the services they had come to render.

One day when the two volunteers were growing a little desperate they heard of a poultry pilot project that had been established at Gurdaspur, Punjab. The project was run by the American foreign aid program, generally referred to as AID. Sean and Bill visited the poultry project and liked what they saw. They were pleased to learn that AID had published a book to help farmers in raising poultry. The young men secured the book, read it, and promptly decided to launch poultry raising around Nabha. In telling later of this rather brash decision, Bill Donovan said, "That was all the background we had and in our ignorance we felt it was all we needed."

The volunteers persuaded a few farmers to start raising poultry. As Bill put it, "From there, things just seemed to snowball. Our project, which started out with a few people, had in a year's time blossomed into thirty farmers and a feed and marketing service, complete with a 1929 Ford Roadster pickup truck."

Before the volunteers' tour of duty ended a group of farmers formed an association to handle the feed and marketing operations. Sean and Bill were thus able to leave the project where it belonged—in the control of the poultry raisers of Nabha.

The poultry project at Nabha was a happy accident, but out of it came an extensive Peace Corps poultry-raising program in India. Peace Corps officials, convinced by the success at Nabha, set up a plan to train volunteers in modern methods of poultry raising. By the end of 1964, Peace Corps poultry projects were operating in seven Indian states and one territory. About half of the volunteers in India were working with poultry. The Peace Corps goal was to have three hundred volunteers promoting poultry projects in India by 1965.

The first purpose of poultry raising was to produce more food for a hungry nation. A second purpose was to provide additional income for the operator, an important value in a poverty-stricken nation.

Hens begin to lay at about six months. Until that time they yield no income to the producer, but during this period they eat a considerable amount of feed and require care. The Peace Corps promoted the plan of confining the chickens in a poultry house equipped for feeding, watering, and nesting the hens. In order to furnish food, housing, and care for the chickens a poultry raiser needed capital. Some Indian states made grants and loans available to poultry raisers, but a very poor man who had no credit might not be considered a good risk for such a loan. For these reasons poultry raising was usually carried on and the profits realized by men who had some means. But the increased food supply did benefit the poor, as well as the more well-to-do people.

One Saturday morning Tom Schrunk and Woody Jewett, Peace Corps volunteers stationed in Jodhpur, in Rajasthan State, were considering what their next move should be. For six months they had been trying to interest the people of the community in raising chickens. They had persuaded, coaxed, and cajoled, but not one flock had been started.

Gregg Brown instructs a man at Bisauli in packing eggs for shipment.

While the young men were reviewing their problem a jeep stopped in front of their living quarters. A man stepped from the jeep, went to their house, and introduced himself as a member of the family of the maharajah, once the ruler of the local princely state. The man then said, "While I was studying at a university in the United States an American showed me great kindness. Because he was so good to me I want to help you who are also Americans."

The two volunteers related their lack of success in starting poultry raising. Out of this interview came an offer by the maharajah's family to set up a model chicken-raising project. All the family members were interested in the project, especially the maharajah's wife, the maharani. After learning about necessary care for chickens, she sent the royal carpenter to build a brooder. He made one from plans provided by Tom and Woody, using teakwood. The carpenter then converted an unused room in the maharajah's palace into a model poultry house.

The volunteers ordered White Leghorn baby chicks from a

commercial hatchery in Bombay. Tom and Woody placed the
chicks in the teakwood brooder and gave them tender care.
After a month in the brooder the chicks were given larger living space in the palace-poultry-house. The maharani assigned
"a royal waiter" to wait upon the chickens. Tom and Woody
trained this man in the proper care of the flock.

The maharani helped Tom and Woody drop serum into the
eyes of each of the five hundred chicks. This was the first step
in vaccinating them against two serious poultry diseases. When
the birds reached the proper age, Tom and Woody completed,
with the use of a needle, the other steps of vaccination.

When the people of Jodhpur learned that the maharajah's
family was raising chickens their interest in poultry raising
took a rapid upward turn. Within a few months ten families
and a private school had established flocks and some twenty-
five hundred chickens were busily scratching in model chicken
houses.

The royal family's support was the key to launching chicken
raising in Jodhpur. Their kindly attitude toward Americans
also made life more pleasant for the volunteers who were entertained at the palace, invited to ride the maharajah's English
thoroughbreds, and introduced to the friends of the royal family. Tom Schrunk said, "I am certainly grateful to that American who befriended the maharajah's relative."

Vijai Singh lived with his wife and children in a large house
in a suburb of Jaipur, in Rajasthan. He was an airplane pilot
instructor who began raising chickens as a hobby, and then
turned his hobby into a business with fourteen hundred birds
in his chicken houses.

Mr. Singh's large house was a convenience. There was always a room available to shelter baby chicks or sick chicks or
the overflow from a crowded chicken house. Every inch of the
back yard was put to use, too. Mr. Singh kept his cow tied
there and sheltered his flocks in two poultry houses.

The older house, built of brick, had a thatch roof, which provided good protection from the hot sun. The house had solid walls about halfway up and chicken wire mesh above. The open walls allowed good cross-ventilation. Mr. Singh had installed automatic feeders and water troughs that could be filled from the outside. He used pottery jars for nests. He kept straw or ground peanut shells on the floor for litter, adding to it from time to time, and turning it to increase bacterial action. When a flock completed its laying period and the birds were sold for meat, the litter was cleaned out and used for fertilizer and clean litter was provided for the next flock of chickens.

Mr. Singh had a contract to supply a large hotel with eggs. He designed an egg crate in which the eggs were delivered. The crate, which held seven hundred eggs, was attached to a bicycle on which Mr. Singh or a helper rode to make the delivery.

Mr. Singh had learned something about raising chickens before the Peace Corps volunteers came to Jaipur. However, he was very thankful to have the benefit of the new methods that the volunteers taught him. He followed approved practices for vaccinating and debeaking his flock, culling out and selling cockerels, keeping exact records of expenses incurred, and keeping laying records for his hens.

Charles Zumbro and Konrad Peterson were the first volunteers to work with poultry in Jaipur. They found that a number of people in the area had household flocks and three men were raising chickens commercially. Mr. Singh, one of these three, was the first poultry raiser to take advantage of the help offered by the Volunteers. Ten months after Charles and Konrad arrived in Jaipur they reported that the community had more than twenty-five flocks with an average of two hundred fifty birds per flock.

David Benson, working in poultry, was the only American at Nawalgarh, in Rajasthan. He was the first volunteer to work in the community. He created a fair amount of interest in poultry raising and after ten months had fifteen flocks established. However, he found several conditions that did not favor success. Only three of the fifteen men with flocks could read, which made it necessary to give all instructions orally. Since David's Hindi was not good there were problems of communication. The poultry raisers lacked any knowledge of bookkeeping. This lack made it necessary for David and the government official concerned with poultry to keep books for them. In spite of certain difficulties, David felt that he had made an impact on Nawalgarh and gained much from working there.

"We drank tea and explained poultry raising," John Piatek said, in describing his first experiences in Bharatpur.

John and Thomas Graham were the first Peace Corps volunteers to serve in the town, where a District Animal Husbandry Officer was stationed. The District Officer supplied the two young men with a list of names of people whom they might interest in poultry raising.

John and Thomas set out on their round of calls. The two volunteers were the only Americans in Bharatpur so their arrival at any house was the occasion for a flutter of excitement. Tea was always offered by the hospitable Indians, while the family gathered, curious to learn the purpose of the volunteers' visit.

A month after their arrival the volunteers had several men committed to go into the poultry business. Anxious to lose no time, they ordered four hundred chicks from the state poultry farm at Jaipur. In spite of promises made by farmers to construct poultry houses rapidly, not one house was done when the chicks arrived. John and Thomas had no choice but to share their house with the four hundred cheeping babies. They installed the chicks in an empty room and mothered them for two months.

Ten months after their arrival in Bharatpur, the volunteers could count ten poultry raisers, with good prospects for other flocks. The volunteers had also helped to start three demonstration poultry farms in other areas and had built a poultry house for a Vocational and Academic High School, where John taught a class in poultry raising. John established a small poultry unit to provide food at a hospital for orphan children. He also aided a group of local college students who built latrines at the bus station as a public service. Thomas set up an exhibit that was the center of attention at the local agricultural fair. Thomas also found satisfaction in teaching a Hindi literacy class.

The volunteers tried to impress prospective poultry raisers with the need to provide good housing for their chickens. Proof that their persuasion was effective was provided by the man who moved his family into a shed and used his house for the chickens.

William Cammack was transferred to Bisauli, in Uttar Pradesh, after some months in another location. Gregg Brown, an earlier volunteer at Bisauli, had started poultry raising in the area. He secured good co-operation from Dr. Brijreman Lavania, a veterinarian who was a member of the Block Development Staff.

When Bill Cammack went to Bisauli he found that the poultry raisers belonged to the Bisauli Poultry Project. This was a service organization, to which Bill and Dr. Lavania gave assistance. The Project held monthly meetings at which the poultry producers received information and acquired experience in cooperation. The Project acted as a marketing agent for eggs which were shipped to a merchant in Delhi. The eggs were weighed, graded, and packed, 360 eggs to a crate, at the small Project office. The egg crates were sent by rickshaw to the railhead, a few miles from Bisauli, and shipped from there to Delhi by train. The Project also handled chicken feed, selling it to the poultry raisers at the lowest possible cost.

The first poultry raiser in the area was Mr. Masicharan, a

farmer living in Bhatpura Village. He built his first chicken house beside his own mud-walled dwelling inside the village wall. His flock did well, so he bought land at the edge of the village, on which he erected two more chicken houses.

Late one afternoon we went to visit Mr. Masicharan. We found Bhatpura to be a mud-walled village of about one thousand people. Its streets were narrow and crooked and deep with dust because it was the dry season. The cows had been brought back to the village for the night and tied beside the doors of their owners. We walked past the mud-walled houses, gaunt and bare of furnishings, on our way to see the new chicken houses. Mr. Masicharan walked beside us. Behind came his wife, his children, and half the village, the crowd increasing steadily as we moved along. At the new poultry houses the villagers watched attentively while Mr. Masicharan explained his poultry operations in halting English. The bright-eyed children crowded about us, curious and eager to talk to us. It seemed at first that we had no common language. Then we discovered that the Indian children had one English word, "OK." With that we carried on a conversation supplemented by gestures on our part and giggles from the children.

Gerald Vallely and Langdon Williams, whose nickname was Bill, served together at Ajmer, in Rajasthan. They were stationed at a government poultry farm, where they had a modest apartment.

Ajmer is more advanced than many Indian cities. Large railroad shops employ eighteen thousand people. Since there is work, there is prosperity. There are also many Christians in Ajmer and they have no objection to eating eggs and chickens, as some Hindus have. For these reasons the government considered the area around Ajmer a suitable place in which to push the production of poultry. The government poultry farm was established and volunteers were requested as part of a crash program in poultry.

Ten months after Jerry and Bill went to Ajmer there were twenty-three poultry raisers in the area, three of whom were large operators. The volunteers thought that other men with means would go into poultry production because it was proving to be a money-making business. The volunteers urged their producers to expand in order not to be squeezed out by the big operators.

The operator of one poultry farm at Ajmer worked in a shoe factory, where signs were frequently used. He believed that if signs were good in a shoe factory they were better in a poultry house. Approaching the farm, we were greeted by a big sign which said, "Behl Poultry Farm, Guided by American Peace Corps." We were stopped at the door by a red and yellow sign reading, "Please wash your feet before stepping in." Inside we could see red and yellow warnings, among them one which said, "Please do not tease the birds."

Jerry and Bill interested the commanding officer of a Central Reserve Police Post in raising chickens. The regiment stationed at the post went into the poultry business, using a stone and mud poultry house erected by the men in their spare time. They contrived brooders from packing crates lined with tin obtained from kerosene cans. Each brooder was heated by electric light bulbs.

The arrival of the first chicks was greeted with eager interest by the policemen. The 360 babies were placed in the brooders and disaster struck. In the first three days thirty of the chicks smothered. When Bill Williams heard the bad news he went at once to the police post and spent the night in the poultry house watching the brooder and adjusting the heat. A volunteer in poultry is called upon to do many things, one of which is sometimes to serve as a "sitter" for baby chicks.

Aiding Education and Health

Excitement rippled through Calingapatnam. On the streets and in the houses the question put by one villager to another on a certain September day, was always, "Have you seen the American?" The more curious, hoping for a glimpse of the stranger, found occasion to walk past the bungalow where the newcomer to the village had found a dwelling place. And when the American's cook went out for the first time to shop for food, he met a volley of inquiries about his new employer.

Very few western people had ever lived in this fishing village on the Bay of Bengal. It was small wonder that the arrival of Peter Ross to live in the village and teach in the village high school was the cause of questions. In 1963 the American Peace Corps volunteer was the only person from a western nation living in Calingapatnam.

The thirty-five hundred people in the village were a friendly lot. They made Peter welcome but they never lost their curiosity about him. His strange ways were a never-ending source of wonder, often discussed at village gatherings. When he first arrived they called him *doora* (boss, gentleman), but he insisted he was not a doora. He acted as if all the people were of equal importance, even speaking respectfully to women and to his students. He seemed to enjoy teaching. Strangest of all, he actually carried his own bags. The village elders shook their heads when they heard of this violation of Indian custom, and murmured sadly, "Too bad! No dignity!"

Peter was presently launched into a program in which he taught mathematics, physics, and English. The textbooks for mathematics and physics were in Telugu, the language of Andra Pradesh State. Peter could read and write Telugu, but he could not speak it well at first, so he often had to use English, which the students did not understand. The language barriers created problems, but Peter's Telugu and the students' English improved.

Peter assigned homework. His students did not prepare their assignments. His inquiry as to why they had not done so brought a torrent of excuses. "We don't get credit on our grades for homework." "Teachers in this school won't grade homework." "Our houses are crowded." "We have no lights at night." "We have no place to do homework."

Peter looked at the earnest young faces. He recalled the houses he had seen in the village. Then he said, "Let's set up centers where you can study. We shall have lights in the centers and you can do your homework there. One center can be at my house and we'll find places for others." Locations were found and study centers were established. Some were lighted by electricity, others by oil lamps. At first only a few students came, but when examination time approached, students crowded the centers.

During his second year in India, Peter Ross taught mathematics at the Hyderabad Public School. The school was provided with substantial buildings, playing fields, a swimming pool, and a large campus. It has high academic standards.

Peter continued to enjoy teaching and decided to make it his life's work. He was able to help one Indian teacher at the Hyderabad school to acquire new techniques. Peter had had graduate training in mathematics and out of his wide knowledge stimulated a new interest in math on the part of the students.

Peter Ross believed that he had helped students in India feel a new respect for teachers. In a country in which teaching did not usually command respect, Peter counted such a change in attitude as a gain.

Henry Gwiazda and Dallas Lankford taught at the Methodist Boys' School in Hyderabad. Henry taught English, Dallas taught physics.

The Methodist Boys' School offers a full course of instruction from grade one through grade twelve. It has thirty-two hundred students, some of whom live in a hostel on the campus, but most of whom are day students. All students pay tuition, but the cost of board in the hostel is kept as low as possible. Since this is a school established by the mission program of the Methodist Church the school authorities want to keep the cost low to permit Christian boys who may be poor to attend. There are a considerable number of them enrolled, though the majority of students are not Christians. The Methodist Boys' School has good academic standards. It is the excellence of its instruction that attracts non-Christians to the Methodist School.

Henry taught tenth-, eleventh-, and twelfth-grade English and helped with programs in the middle school. He also helped to coach high school basketball. Henry was an active young

Indian students receive corrected papers from a volunteer teacher.

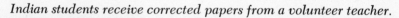

man, bubbling with ideas and energy. He was enthusiastic about his students, whom he described as eager to learn.

In spite of Henry's satisfaction in his own assignment, he did not think that a volunteer's greatest contribution was usually made through the immediate task that he performed. As Henry put it, "I don't think that the Peace Corps can do much for the over-all development of India. But the Peace Corps can help Indians understand the United States and it can help Americans understand India. Both are important."

Dallas enjoyed his teaching, but like many volunteers teaching in schools subject to external examinations he thought there was too much emphasis upon memorizing. Dallas said, "The students are either unable or unwilling to use problem solving. They want the teacher to work the problem on the blackboard. They then copy and memorize the solution."

Dallas taught a high school Sunday school class for Christian boys living in the hostel. From time to time he helped groups of boys produce plays and programs for special occasions.

Sibyl Baeszler taught courses in child development and textiles at the College of Home Science in Hyderabad. She had a room in the student hostel. The student girls dropped in to see Sibyl and often borrowed books from her. They invited her to their homes and through this means she developed a wide circle of contacts with local people.

The College of Home Science was established as a government institution. It was later made a part of Rajunedarager College of Agriculture, which has a campus near Hyderabad. When its new building on the agricultural college campus is completed, the College of Home Science will move there from its present location. Sibyl traveled over India, visiting nearly all the other colleges giving work in home science to gain ideas for new courses to be offered on the new campus.

Change was the order of the day at the college. External

examinations were giving way to examinations prepared by the instructors. Group discussion was supplementing lectures in Sibyl's classes. Students were performing tasks as part of their classwork which they had never done in their homes. These tasks included cooking, cleaning, scrubbing, washing, and ironing. When the new building was completed and a nursery school was installed, the students would also care for young children. These changes, accepted by the students in good spirit, were of special significance in India, where there is scant respect or little liking for manual labor.

Sibyl Baeszler found that after she became their friend the students were receptive to her ideas. This experience led her to remark, "Before the Peace Corps, or any outside group, can bring about changes in India, there must be mutual trust and understanding."

Lorus Hawbecker had five years experience in psychiatric nursing before she joined the Peace Corps. She was assigned to the College of Nursing in Hyderabad, where she and an Indian co-worker organized a period of study and practice in psychiatric nursing. The two worked under the supervision of an adviser provided through the American AID program.

The course opened with a series of lectures concerning the care of the mentally ill given to the student nurses. At the end of the lectures the students were divided into groups of eight, for work in a local mental hospital, four hours per day, six days per week. Lorus gave close supervision to four girls, her co-worker dealt in a similar way with the other four in the group. The groups followed each other, until all the student nurses had had the experience at the mental hospital.

While at the hospital the student nurses were responsible for the physical care, physical treatment, and recreation of patients. The purpose of the course that Lorus helped to organize was to give the student a concept of the patient as an individual and to give basic instruction in the nature and care of psychiatric illness.

Lorus, small, blond, dynamic, and articulate, pointed out a basic difference between the focus of nursing in the United States and in India. She said, "I was trained to make the patient my primary concern. Here in the College of Nursing the student nurse, not the patient, is the primary concern."

Ann Bullion created a job for herself. Ann was a licensed practical nurse with several years' experience when she joined the Peace Corps. While nursing at the mental hospital Ann saw that the recreation program needed to be organized. She asked for and received authority to carry out such a program. When the student nurses finished their assignments at the hospital, Ann went into action. She scrounged for equipment and materials and made weekly schedules for the employed occupational therapy staff. The patients responded with eager enthusiasm. The job that Ann created because she saw an unmet need grew until it took her full time. The patients benefited, and Ann Bullion found a way to be both useful and happy as a volunteer.

Joanne Sivertson was also a licensed practical nurse serving as a volunteer in Hyderabad. She began her Peace Corps work at Niloufer Hospital. She found such a wide difference between the ideas that she held about nursing and the procedures followed in the hospital that she asked for a transfer. She was assigned to the Niloufer Public Health School, where she helped to train girls to serve in Indian villages as health workers.

For a part of her training period each student worked either in a maternal and child health center in a city or in a primary health unit in a village. At the center she learned to apply her knowledge of sanitation, nutrition, and other aspects of health. Joanne's responsibility was to supervise the students at the center and to go with them on home calls to see if the patients had followed instructions given at the center. Joanne's work gave her close personal contact with the students, mothers, and children. In spite of difficulties in communication caused by language differences, many of them became Joanne's good friends and a source of satisfaction to her.

Victoria Rodefeld, a mature woman with considerable experience as a registered nurse, was assigned to Osmania General Hospital in Hyderabad. This is the largest hospital in Andra Pradesh, with beds for one thousand patients. But the hospital often has fifteen hundred patients, with pallets spread on the floors in corridors. Added to this number are the family members who go along to care for the patients, as is the custom in many parts of Asia and Africa.

Virginia and three other nurse volunteers set up a model ward at Osmania Hospital. The head nurse in the ward was pleased with this service, but Virginia felt that the other ward nurses and some of the doctors resisted the new ideas introduced by the volunteers. Virginia later asked for and received a transfer to the Osmania School of Nursing. Virginia said, "I do not think that volunteers can change nursing practices in the hospitals, but I hope by instilling a conscience in student nurses we may lift nursing practices in the future."

Jon and Dorothy Nyberg spent their first months in India at Tonk. Jon taught English and Dorothy was the only nurse in a government hospital. Jon found his lack of fluency in Urdu a handicap. Dorothy expected to teach new techniques to Indian nurses but there were no other nurses. Such care as patients received was given by members of their families who went with them to the hospital. Neither Jon nor Dorothy felt fulfilled by their duties at Tonk. They asked for a transfer and were sent to Madar Union Sanitorium near Ajmer, in Rajasthan.

Jon was designated business manager and overseer at the Sanitorium, but he turned his hand to a variety of duties. Dorothy was placed in charge of the Recovery Room and Intensive Care area. A schedule was planned that permitted her to work in shifts with all the nurses on the staff, training them in the latest techniques. She also taught a class made up of nurses from other mission hospitals in the area.

Madar Union Sanitorium is a Methodist mission project for tubercular patients. It is open to patients from all parts of India. The hospital handles many tubercular cases requiring surgery. It has, in addition to the main hospital building, cottages for convalescent patients, a kitchen and dining hall, a chapel, and quarters for its staff. Jon and Dorothy occupied a staff cottage. Dorothy and Jon had a deeply satisfying experience at the Madar Union Sanitorium.

Before independence there was little health service available to the Indian people living in the villages. After independence a system of rural health service was established. Under the plan a primary health center was located in each development block. A medical officer headed each primary health center and was assisted by a staff of health workers. People in the block went to the center for examination, treatment, and other health services.

Dr. Mohd Ghousuddin was the medical officer in charge of Narsingi Primary Health Center in Andra Pradesh. The Center served five villages, the most distant being five miles away from Narsingi. Dr. Ghousuddin visited each village once a month and answered calls at other times. There were about two hundred families in the five villages. Two volunteer nurses had assigned duties at Narsingi.

The Center, housed in a neat building, provided a doctor's office, a sterilizing room, two wards each with three beds, a delivery room, a room where dressings were applied, a family welfare room, and a health museum. The latter was equipped with posters, models, and other visual aids designed to teach health lessons. The Center had electricity but no running water. Its only sanitary facility was an outdoor latrine.

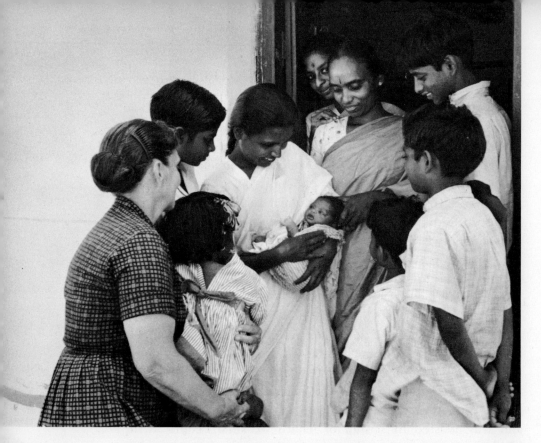

Frances Larrson, Peace Corps volunteer nurse in India, admires a new baby during a home call made with a student nurse in Narsingi.

Dr. Ghousuddin's staff included a compounder, who dispensed medicines, a health inspector, who checked sources of contamination, two health visitors, who worked on family planning and maternal and child care, four midwives, who delivered babies, a worker called the *ayah,* who applied dressings, and several peons who cleaned and ran errands.

Frances Larrson, a Peace Corps volunteer, worked with students from the College of Nursing in Hyderabad who were training at Narsingi to become health visitors in the villages. The students went to Narsingi in groups, each group staying three months. They lived in a house near the Primary Health Center and used a second building nearby for classroom purposes. During their period at Narsingi the students attended classes taught by a lecturer from the College of Nursing staff and made home calls under Frances Larrson's guidance.

Narsingi Village had a primary school. The school building had three small rooms but there were 165 children enrolled, divided into five classes. One class met in the shade of the building and another met under a tree. The children of Muslim parents attended a class for grades one, two, and three, taught in the Urdu tongue. There were two sections of first graders and two sections of second graders who were taught in Telugu, the official language of Andra Pradesh State.

The children sat on the floor or ground, their slates and such books as they had spread in the dust. One of the rooms had a small blackboard and chart. There were neither toilet facilities nor sources of water at the school.

This school, like many in India, had the Midday Meal Feeding Program using food provided by CARE. The food consisted of powdered milk, cornmeal, and butter.

A Peace Corps volunteer nurse, Linda Salsman, was assigned to set up a school health program for the five villages connected with the Primary Health Center at Narsingi. An immediate responsibility that fell to Linda in Narsingi Village was the coordination of the Midday Meal Feeding Program.

Linda secured a place to cook and serve the food on the porch of a public building in Narsingi. A fire was built there each morning and the cook placed a big kettle of water to boil in preparation for making the mush. While the water heated the cook mixed the milk, beating it to dissolve lumps with a beater that Linda had contrived from salvaged wire.

In the meantime, a teacher at the school sent boys to bring water from a well half a mile away. The pupils filed past a boy who dipped water from a jar and dribbled it over their hands. After this effort at hand washing, the children walked to the porch, where the mush was bubbling in the big kettle. Linda handed out plastic bowls, the children lined up and filed past

the cook, who ladled mush into their bowls. As soon as it was
cool enough to eat the children plunged into it, eating with
their right hands as is the custom in Indian villages. When the
mush was gone Linda and the cook poured the milk and the
children polished off their meal with big bowls of milk.

Linda had participated in a village pilot project carried out
by the Peace Corps. This project was operated to test and
evaluate a technique for instructing primary teachers in matters pertaining to health. In the project a team consisting of
five volunteers gave intensive instruction for one month in an
institution which trained primary teachers. On the team were
three home economists, one agricultural worker, and one nurse
—the latter being Linda. Peace Corps officials studied the
evaluations of the pilot project and approved it for future use
in other training centers for primary teachers. One aspect of
health work stressed in the pilot project was the Midday Meal
Feeding Program, which can be expected to spread when the
new training program is in operation.

When first established, the nursing program in India encountered difficulties which stemmed from several causes. The
difference in the status of nursing in India and America was
one cause. In India nursing is not as respected a profession as
it is in America. The differences in emphasis and practice in
Indian and American hospitals was another cause of friction.
A lack of tact upon the part of some Peace Corps nurses who
were too eager to make changes in Indian hospitals probably
created resentment among Indian nurses. The sensitivities of a
newly independent people may have been a factor.

Nursing has not been abandoned in the Indian Peace Corps
program. But in the future the nursing volunteers will be
placed in situations where they can succeed and render assistance to India in her valiant effort to improve the health of her
people.

Increasing Mechanical Skills and Services

Jay Klinck watched a mechanic grinding a valve. As the mechanic finished the operation Jay glanced at his watch. When the grinding was completed Jay checked the time again, then moved across the machine shop to a workbench where another man was grinding a valve. Once more he timed the operation.

Presently Jay called the group of mechanics together. "I have been watching the way you grind valves," he said. "It takes you about eleven minutes to grind one valve. I am going to show you how to do the same job in three minutes."

The men watched intently while Jay demonstrated his technique. When he completed the job quickly, as he had promised, they smiled at his evident satisfaction in the accomplishment.

"You see how much faster it is, don't you?" Jay inquired.

All the heads nodded in agreement.

"Of course you'll want to use this method hereafter, because it saves so much time," Jay concluded.

The men weighed this typically American comment for a few seconds. Then one of them said, "But if I grind the valve more quickly, I'll just have to do that many more."

This exchange between an American Peace Corps volunteer and an Indian mechanic illustrates the difference in patterns of thought prevailing in the United States and India. To an American, time is to be saved; to an Indian, time is endless.

Jay Klinck liked to tinker with motors. During his high school years he and a friend spent endless hours working on cars. Jay disliked school almost as much as he liked motors, so he quit high school and joined the Peace Corps. But he was "selected out" during training and advised to finish high school and, if still interested, to apply again to the Peace Corps.

The boy returned to high school. He did not like it any better than before, but he wanted to join the Peace Corps so much that he disciplined himself and remained until he graduated. He again entered the Peace Corps and after training was sent to India to serve as a mechanic.

Jay was first sent to Ahmedabad, in Gujarat State, where he served with two other volunteer mechanics. The volunteers had two assignments at Ahmedabad, to repair vehicles provided by UNICEF for doctors and nurses serving in the primary health centers and to train local mechanics.

The three volunteers had a good experience at Ahmedabad. They trained fifteen local men who were very responsive to the instruction. After a few months the volunteers felt that the men had made so much progress that the vehicle repair could be left to them. The Peace Corps then transferred the volunteers to new locations, arranging for one of them to go back at intervals to give further help, if it were needed.

Jay was sent to Hyderabad, in Andra Pradesh, to a similar job. However, he found more problems there, for the repair shop was disorganized and fifty-two vehicles belonging to the health service were awaiting attention. Jay opened crates of spare parts provided earlier by AID but not yet in use, organized a spare-parts room, designed a form to be used in making inventories of vehicles, set up an inventory control record, and started a training class for local mechanics. Later he added to his duties the instruction of the mechanics in English and the teaching of a class in automotive technology for a local polytechnic college.

The mechanics were eager to learn both English and technical skills. Jay worked beside them and found them friendly and cooperative. It seemed likely that the fifty-two vehicles would be repaired before Jay's tour of duty ended.

When we discussed a schedule with Mr. Ashabranner he said that we must visit the workshop at Bisauli. Since this town in Uttar Pradesh State was remote from public transportation we hired a private car and driver and set out early one morning from New Delhi. The driver did not know the way, and the road map was poorly marked, but as long as the road signs were in English we kept on the right course. Our troubles began when the use of English ceased and the infrequent road signs were all in Hindi. Our driver could read English and Punjabi, but not Hindi. And neither could we.

The wonder was not that we arrived at Bisauli an hour late, but that we arrived at all. The volunteers welcomed us warmly and were not surprised to learn that we had taken some wrong turns. They, too, had been lost on the winding, poorly marked road that led to Bisauli.

The four volunteers stationed in Bisauli at the time of our visit were Stephen Thompson, Eric Hodges, and Tom Wick, all of whom were at the workshop, and Bill Cammack, whose assignment was in poultry raising. The young men had a house and a competent houseman who cooked and directed the operation of the household. Jay Klinck, who was having his annual vacation, was visiting the volunteers in Bisauli when we were there.

The young men knew that we were to be their guests and had made preparations for us. Two freshly made Indian beds awaited us in the bedroom. The cook carried in big platters of American-style fried chicken and other delicacies prepared in our honor.

The volunteers took us to see their various projects. They told us of their problems and achievements. They invited the local veterinarian, Dr. Brijreman Lavania, a close associate of Bill

Cammack in poultry promotion, to spend the evening with us. Dr. Lavania had a good command of English and an acute awareness of India's current problems. Our conversation with him was most rewarding.

The workshop at Bisauli was established in 1962 to repair tools and farm implements. Officials at the Agricultural University in Uttar Pradesh conceived the idea of the workshop after the University was assigned the responsibility for doing agricultural extension work in three development blocks in the state. The officials found an abandoned court house in Bisauli which could be used to house the workshop.

Two Peace Corps volunteers, Glenn and Anne Elkins, were assigned the task of establishing a repair shop in this building. Glenn had been a high school history teacher. Anne was a nurse. Neither had had any experience in repairing tools, but as volunteers they could be expected to attempt the nearly impossible, so off they went to Bisauli.

The volunteers took over the courthouse from the monkeys, pigeons, and cows that had been living in it, cleaned the building, and whitewashed the interior. The Agricultural University and AID both made loans and grants available for establishing the workshop. Glenn Elkins used the funds to install electricity, purchase some machines, and hire a skilled repair man. By late 1962 the Bisauli workshop was ready for business.

The farmers brought their simple plows to have the iron tips renewed. The few bicycles of the community were all put in good working order. Still the repairman was not fully occupied and Glenn realized that operations must be expanded in order to put the project on a firm financial footing. He decided that the workshop should try to make new farm implements. He secured certain implements from the United States to serve as guides for developing simpler ones suited to agricultural conditions in Uttar Pradesh. Skilled blacksmiths were employed and the work of making agricultural implements was launched.

Three new volunteers were added as the project developed.

None had had experience in a machine shop, but John Stettler and James Limburg were trained in agriculture. The third volunteer, Joe Pena, had worked in a gas station.

The workshop had some power machines. The volunteers trained local men to use these, but the greater part of the work of making the implements was done by hand. The Indian blacksmiths were skilled and resourceful craftsmen.

The workshop turned out land-levelers, wheel hoes, and three-tined cultivators. The latter tool was used for both plowing and cultivating. These implements were more efficient than those commonly used by farmers in Uttar Pradesh. The men on the block development teams who were concerned with agricultural improvement demonstrated the new implements and promoted their sale to local farmers.

In May 1963, the workshop incorporated under the laws of Uttar Pradesh as a production co-operative. This step had three

Volunteer Joe Pena repairs equipment at the Bisauli workshop.

advantages. It involved local people, who bought shares in the co-operative, in the project. It put the venture in a position to secure the financial assistance permitted by the government to co-operatives, and it established legal ownership.

Community leaders backed the production co-operative. An executive committee was elected and prospects for success seemed high. However, problems, common to many co-operative ventures in India, soon arose. The people had very little mutual trust or experience in co-operation, the executive committee did not like to take responsibility for making decisions, and the members did not work harmoniously together.

Soon after the co-operative was formed, a district official in Uttar Pradesh asked Glenn Elkins to develop an efficient and moderately priced device for lifting water in the wells which dot the great plain in north India. The water was commonly lifted to the surface in small buckets attached to a continuous chain. A more efficient device had been invented but it was expensive The volunteers set to work on this problem and produced an efficient device that could be sold at a moderate price.

The new device is called a *washer rahet*. It consists of two parts: a stationary pipe, five and a half inches in diameter, which is placed in the well, and a moving chain on which washers are fastened, which passes through the pipe and lifts the water to the surface. The power is provided, as in the older type of well, by animals that tread a path while harnessed to the water wheel. With the washer rahet more water is lifted with the same expenditure of animal energy than is possible with the bucket-type device.

The block development workers demonstrated the water rahet and explained its advantages. In the first year of its production the cooperative sold some two hundred water rahets.

The Bisauli Co-operative Workshop was a boon to the community. During the peak months of production it employed ninety to a hundred men. In off-season it gave work to about sixteen men. In addition to employing blacksmiths and machinists, the workshop also used some carpenters who turned out poultry brooders and feeders.

A regular training program for machinists and carpenters was developed at the workshop which trained four men at a time over a period of forty-two days. By the end of its second year, the workshop had trained forty men in this program. Both volunteers and the more skilled Indian craftsmen acted as instructors for the training.

The volunteers who pioneered in the development of the workshop and its conversion into a co-operative venture completed their tours of duty. They were replaced at Bisauli by Stephen, Eric, and Tom, who also took over the house occupied by the earlier volunteers.

Stephen Thompson, who arrived in January 1964, functioned as the new business manager and leader of the project. Steve had completed three years of college with accounting as his major. He had minors in economics and business management. This background of study combined with a pleasant, outgoing personality fitted Steve to act in the jobs that he assumed.

When Eric Hodges arrived in Bisauli he was made inside foreman. He later became general foreman of the workshop. Eric knew nothing about blacksmithing when he went to Bisauli, but he discovered that an Indian blacksmith is a creative person who has pride in his skills. Eric learned blacksmithing from his Indian coworkers and found working in metal a satisfying form of self expression.

Tom Wick was sent to Bisauli because he was a graduate in mechanical engineering. He functioned at the workshop as an engineer, designing a new type of cultivator, running an inventory on materials, supervising installations of the water rahet, and inspecting earlier installations to learn how these were functioning.

Tom enjoyed his work and he felt that he was gaining valuable engineering experience. However he joined the Peace Corps because he wanted to help people and he thought he might feel more rewarded if his job offered opportunity for person-to-person assistance.

When the Bisauli Productive Cooperative ended its business year on June 30, 1964, it had made a profit of 13,700 rupees (about $2,870). It had repaid all loans that had come due and had the funds to pay outstanding loans when they were due. It had reinvested more than three thousand rupees in the plant and in raw materials. It had paid the shareholders the maximum dividend permitted by law. In such a state of prosperity there would seem to be no problems, but there were problems. One concerned management, the other ownership.

The Peace Corps believed that the workshop had proved its value, but it also believed that local people should take over the management, thus releasing volunteers for other duties. Soon after our visit the cooperative employed an Indian manager. Stephen, Eric, and Tom were given new assignments in Uttar Pradesh state. The workshop continued to flourish. Six months after the Indian manager took over his duties he reported that his most serious problem was to get materials to keep up with the many orders received at the workshop.

In Bisauli, as well as in other places visited in India, we felt that the work of the Peace Corps had a value beyond the immediate materials produced and skills taught. Even more important than these worthy achievements was the effect of the Peace Corps work in changing the attitude of the people. Mr. Ashabranner put the matter well when he said, "More vital than producing a million eggs is what the volunteers can do in making people realize that new things can be tried, new goals set and achieved."

Our young hosts at Bisauli and several hundred other Peace Corps volunteers are changing attitudes. In an ancient land they are indeed kindlers of the spark.

6. AT WORK IN MALAYSIA

An Experiment in Federation

The Malay Peninsula is a bridge connecting the Asian mainland with the great sweep of islands to the south and east. For centuries people migrated from the Asian mainland over this land bridge, some to settle in the peninsula, many more to push farther to the islands beyond.

The Malayan bridge proved to be more than a causeway over which people passed to new locations. It was also a command post which secured for its occupants control of the trade routes over which goods passed. And because this was true, peoples contested with each other through centuries for possession of the peninsula and its fringe islands.

In the sixteenth century the Portuguese, Dutch, and British competed for control of strategic points in the area in order to profit from trade. The British secured for their use three important ports, Penang, Singapore, and Malacca, and formed them into a colony called the Straits Settlements. The Malay Peninsula and the northern part of the island of Borneo also came within the British sphere of influence. It was the union of these several areas, once under British influence or control, that created the Federation of Malaysia in 1963.

Through the centuries of migrations and political changes, the area that was to become Malaysia received people of different races who came from many lands and practiced many religions. Today in the rich diversity of the Malaysian people one can see the mark left by that great procession of peoples who traversed the area.

The peninsula which is called Malaya is divided by a mountain range running in a north–south direction. The larger centers of population are along the coasts, most of them on the west coast. The British built roads and railroads, thus opening new areas to settlement.

Singapore Island lies off the southern tip of the peninsula. It has a wide river and an excellent harbor. The city of Singapore, which grew up around the harbor, has developed into one of the great ports of the modern world.

The largest part of the area in Borneo that was once in the British sphere of influence is now included in two states called Sarawak and Sabah. These states have a coastal plain which rises to hills and rugged mountains in the interior. The rivers are wide and winding. The jungles are dense and the roads are few.

The entire area lies close to the equator. Rainfall is very heavy and the temperatures are high during the day. The heat, combined with the great humidity, makes the days oppressive. The nights are cooler and more pleasant.

Soon after the Second World War ended, the British began to prepare Malaya for self-government. However, the movement for independence in Malaya was delayed by the struggle to prevent Communists from taking over the country. The Malayans had to ferret out Communist guerillas and deal with Communist-inspired strikes, arson, and murder. The bitter struggle went on for twelve years, but it finally brought victory over the Communists in 1960. In the meantime, on August 31, 1957, the Federation of Malayia, made up of the states in the peninsula, had attained independence under the leadership of Prime Minister Abdul Rahman.

Singapore had a large measure of self-government in the postwar years, but it too had economic problems and Communist agitators. The Prime Minister of Singapore, Lee Kuan Yew, proposed the merger of Singapore with the Federation of Malaya. This proposal did not at first find favor with Abdul Rahman because Singapore had a very large Chinese population, while

Malaya had a majority of Malays. The Prime Minister of Malaya did not wish his country to enter a merger that would place the Malays in a minority position.

Presently a new element was added, with the possibility that the states in British Borneo might also become part of the merger. After two years of negotiation, the Federation of Malaysia was established on September 16, 1963, as an independent nation. The new Federation was formed by joining Malaya, Singapore, Sarawak, and Sabah. The small state of Brunei, the remaining part of British Borneo, was invited to join the Federation, but it refused to do so. The Malays and other native peoples of Sabah and Sarawak formed 46 per cent of the population. The Chinese formed 43 per cent, Indians and Pakistanis 9 per cent, and people from other areas 2 per cent.

The Federation was made up of fourteen states with the Prime Minister acting as the head of government. Abdul Rahman became the first Prime Minister of Malaysia. The ceremonial head of state is called the Yang di-Pertuan Agong, which means paramount ruler or chief of state. The paramount ruler has no real power. His most important function is to serve as a symbol of unity in the nation. The federal capital of Malaysia is Kuala Lumpur.

The new Federation faced two serious problems. The first was an internal problem, resulting from differences that existed within the Federation. It was made up of four regions whose people differed in economic and social advancement, in race, language, religion, and cultural habits. The Malays and the Chinese were rivals, with the Chinese often forging ahead economically. To offset this the Malays received, as the price of their consent to federation, political advantages that were resented by the Chinese.

The external problem which threatened the Federation almost from its beginning was the aggression of Indonesia. Britain has a mutual defense treaty with the Federation of Malaysia. President Sukarno of Indonesia seized on this as a reason to oppose the Federation of Malaysia, calling the Federation an effort to keep alive British influence in the area.

In Borneo where Indonesia and Malaysia share a common border of nearly a thousand miles, Indonesian guerrillas have made constant raids into Malaysian territory. Britain has honored her agreement with Malaysia and has sent troops to man the border and contain the Indonesians.

Armed groups of Indonesians landed on Malaya and Singapore Island, explaining when captured that they came to "liberate" the Malaysians from British colonialism. Sharp fighting by Malaysian and British forces, the capture of Indonesians who escaped to the jungles, and the destruction of some Indonesian boats as they approached have protected Malaya and Singapore, but the aggression continues.

Trade has always been a great factor in the prosperity of Singapore and some of the smaller ports as well. When the Indonesians began to harass the Malaysians, the Federation ended trade with Indonesia. Since Indonesia had bought heavily in Malaysia, this move hurt Malaysian business, especially in Singapore.

The leaders who had formed the Federation hoped that they could mold the four regions and several racial groups into one nation. The economy was prosperous and developing. Rubber production was good. High quality tin was mined and smelted. Iron ore, bauxite, coal, ilmenite, and manganese were produced. Rice growing was expanding, and new plantings of oil palms and pineapples were providing cash crops.

The leaders believed that in federation they had found a key to unity in diversity. But deep-seated rivalries and economic pressures proved stronger than the obvious advantages of unity. In August 1965, the Malaysian Prime Minister, Abdul Rahman, demanded that Singapore withdraw from the Federation. With reluctance, Singapore did so. A campaign by Lee Kuan Yew,

Prime Minister of Singapore, to end certain political restrictions upon the Chinese in Malaysia had alarmed some of the Malays and led to the break. The restrictions upon the Chinese included the establishment of Malay as the official national language, and a voting system so weighted as to assure Malay control of the Malaysian central government in Kuala Lumpur.

The Federation, now consisting of Malaya, Sabah, and Sarawak, proposes to live at peace with Singapore and to continue to resist the aggression of Indonesia. What the future holds for the Federation and for Singapore, only time will tell. Impressive economic and social reforms had been achieved under Lee Kuan Yew's leadership in Singapore before the split. The Federation had started a drive to end illiteracy throughout the nation and to increase facilities for education. The number of children in school had steadily increased. Universities, schools for technical, agricultural, and teacher training had been provided, and an extensive adult education program had been launched. Malaysia had also developed a rural health plan and built hospitals in the larger centers of population.

Singapore's withdrawal from the Federation has no immediate implications for the Peace Corps, because no volunteers were serving in Singapore. Peace Corps activities in Malaya, Sarawak, and Sabah continue.

We traveled in Malaysia by plane and car, following a schedule arranged by the Peace Corps staff, headed by Mr. James Gould, Peace Corps Representative for Malaysia. We visited classrooms, health centers, libraries, hospitals, and resettlement projects, and were entertained in a Malaysian home.

Training Young Minds

When Dr. and Mrs. V. A. Subramaniam of Malacca learned from their Peace Corps friend, Robert Highfill, that we were to be in their city they planned a party to welcome us. Dr. Subramaniam, who is both a veterinarian and a minister of the Methodist Church, had twice gone to the United States for professional study. His young daughter had recently spent a year there as an exchange student under the American Field Service Program. The family had an affectionate regard for the United States.

The guests whom we met at the party included the Peace Corps volunteers serving in the area and a number of friends and relatives of the Subramaniams. With gentle courtesy, the Malaysians made all of us from America feel welcome. We were soon answering the many questions put to us and asking some of our own.

When Mrs. Subramaniam led us to the dining room we found a buffet table spread with Malaysian delicacies that whetted both our appetites and our curiosity. There were steamed rice flour patties, considered "company food" in Malaysia. There was rice, and to be eaten with it both curried chicken and a cubed meat dish made with a hot pepper sauce. Cabbage, a fruit and vegetable salad, and a number of other dishes were prepared by Malaysian recipes, but the "icebox" dessert was an American dish, served by the hostess as a compliment to her American guests.

After dinner Dr. Subramaniam spoke of his student days in the United States and of his daughter's later experiences there. He expressed the gratitude that he felt to Americans for all that had been done for him and his family.

The evening in the Subramaniam home was a pleasant occasion. We were grateful for the privilege of being a guest at the party and we appreciated the new understanding of Malaysian life that the party afforded us.

Robert Highfill, who had had both graduate work and teaching experience in mathematics, taught at Malacca High School. Like all government schools in Malaysia, this one was organized on the British plan. Robert taught math, mostly to sixth form students. This is the highest level, or grade, in a British-type secondary school. The students who reach the sixth form, by surviving the rigid examinations that are a feature of the British system, are apt to be capable in academic subjects. Robert found that this was the case with his students.

"I have the best assignment in the Peace Corps," was Robert's enthusiastic evaluation of his teaching situation. He enumerated the good features of his position as including capable, well-disciplined students, co-operative fellow teachers, and a headmaster with whom he had pleasant relations.

Malacca High School had one thousand students. The school offered a wide variety of sports and clubs. Its superior science program enabled students to win science scholarships. It had libraries, including one for sixth form students, that contained some four thousand books.

In spite of its superior features, Malacca High School offered no work in the "new math." Robert deplored this lack and was eager to help achieve a modern math program. He had found a local teacher who shared his enthusiasm. The two men had made plans to offer during the next term a course for upper secondary school teachers in the area. Robert thought that this course in the introduction to numbers might provide the opening wedge for a new program.

A number of teachers were among the volunteers at the party. Two of them, Robert and Mary Dendy, had arrived only two months before. Mary had not yet been given a schedule at the Malacca Girls' High School where she would teach. Robert was settled into a math and science program at Gajah Berang Secondary School.

The school used English as the medium of instruction, but in Malaysia English is spoken with a British accent. Some of the schoolboys had difficulty understanding Robert's English, spoken with an American accent. However, he found that the students who attended American movies or saw the taped American TV shows understood him quite well.

Commenting on student behavior, Robert said, "The boys are always horsing around." After a moment he added, "They are just like American students."

Dan and Nancy Tunstall, teaching at Jasin, near Malacca, were also party guests. They had been nearly a year in Malaysia. Nancy, red-haired and animated, found it stimulating and interesting to live in Malaysia, even though she taught in a crowded double-shift school and lived in cramped quarters. Nancy taught English and Dan taught science at Jasin Secondary English School, which enrolled one thousand students, but had only one small building. The Jasin community had Malays, Chinese, and Indians. Nancy and Dan tried to maintain contacts with all three racial communities, but they found that their various acquaintances and friends did not know each other, because racial groups in Malaysia do not usually mix.

Alan Olson, teaching his second year at Tunku Besar Secondary School in Tampin, was an electrical engineer who had always wanted to teach. He found the British system of education discouraging in its effect upon student creativity and interest, but he thought he might enjoy teaching in America. He liked the boys and enjoyed helping with the school's sports program, especially kickball. In speaking of this popular sport, Alan said, "The way Malaysians use their feet is fantastic." Then he added ruefully, "My ankles don't flop the way Malaysian ankles do."

Alan did not think that a complete change to the American system of education would meet Malaysia's needs, but he did believe that the gap between the standard of performance expected and student ability should be narrowed. However, Alan was optimistic about the future. In this connection, he said, "The Malaysians are broadening the base of their educational program. There is real interest in this country in more education. I think that is the hope of this nation."

Katherine Connerty and Sharon Furrow lived together in an apartment on the campus of the Malay Women's Training College in Malacca. Kay taught science and geography at the college, which trained primary teachers for Malay medium schools. Kay found that the primary schools were giving less emphasis to examinations and were introducing modern methods and equipment. Her students lacked the initiative and imagination she had found in American students, but they worked hard and were eager to learn.

The college at Malacca is the only women's college training primary teachers in which the students live on the campus. Kay discovered that the rules governing the social life of the women students were strict. They could be off the campus only to take part in college-sponsored activities and were always carefully chaperoned by the teachers. The students had parties on the campus, but no men could be invited to the parties.

Sharon Furrow taught English and Art in Yok Bin National Type Secondary School in Malacca. Originally a Mandarin Chinese school, Yok Bin had recently been made an English medium school. Though the school was coeducational, Sharon's students were all boys and all Chinese. They used only the Chinese language outside of school, so spoken English was not easy for them. However, they worked hard on the areas tested by examinations.

The students often asked Sharon how they differed from American students. Sharon thought they differed decidedly in

Robert Weakley helps a Technical College student in Kuala Lumpur.

one way. As she put it, "The students here never question authority."

Sharon was pleased to find as the year advanced that her older students were asking more questions. This was a change in attitude because Malaysian students are inclined to think that asking questions may be construed as criticism of the teacher.

An extra activity that engaged Sharon's free time was working with girls at a local reform school. She taught an English class and, as opportunity permitted, took groups of the girls on short outings, helped them with sewing, and in other ways tried to be friendly and kind.

Four Peace Corps volunteers taught in Seremban. Jo Ann Isackson was at the Day Training Center in Seremban, a training school for primary teachers. There she lectured in educational psychology, supervised practice teachers, and helped prepare a new syllabus for the psychology course. Jo Ann taught music to orphans as an extra service. She was happy at Seremban, but she was dubious about the value of her work because she could not point out specific accomplishments.

Lorraine Stewart was a tiny young woman whose Standard 5E boys and girls at King George V Primary School sometimes towered above her. Lorraine loved the bright-eyed, friendly, rowdy children in 5E and they returned her love.

Commenting on her daily battle to maintain discipline, Lorraine said, "The children are my friends, but they are not afraid of me, and I can't bring myself to shame them or to cuff them as is usual here."

The organization of primary education made teaching these children all but impossible. In Malaysia the classes are divided into academic ability groups, called "streams." The brightest children are in A stream, those in the next ability group are in B stream, and so on. Standard 5E stream was composed of children in Standard 5 with low academic ability. Yet they were given exactly the same lessons as were the children in A stream and were expected to pass the same examinations. It was in no way surprising to Lorraine that the children failed on every examination.

Clifford and Margaret Cook had a Peace Corps romance which culminated in a wedding in Hawaii at the end of their training in the Islands. In Seremban, Clifford, an experienced teacher, taught English and Art at Chan Wa National Type Secondary School. This was an English medium school, but nearly all the students were Chinese. The school offered only four forms so the crucial examinations were taken at the end of the fourth form. Clifford, like every other volunteer teaching under this system, was unhappy over the demands that all instruction be by lecture and all learning be by memorizing. He created both oral and written exercises to combat this and found younger students responsive, but fourth formers had little interest beyond getting down notes.

Clifford made contacts with his students outside of class to extend their limited experiences. He sponsored a guitar group. He took boys on hikes into the jungle. He and Margaret took a bus load of students on a four-day trip in which they slept on schoolhouse floors and ate at roadside stalls and markets. Those four days and nights put the Cooks to bed, but they greatly extended the students' knowledge of their own country.

Margaret Cook had had graduate training in science and two years of college teaching before she joined the Peace Corps. She taught biological science in King George V Secondary School. This was a six-form school, the only one in the state.

The teachers in the school circulated from room to room. The biology teachers had access to the biological laboratory only at intervals and often not when it could most aid instruction. This situation was one of several vexations that Margaret experienced. She was unhappy because she had not been assigned to teach the highest ability groups. She was disappointed because she was not permitted to take students on field trips. Margaret was glad to be teaching in Malaysia, but she thought that, if she were given the opportunity, she could render more valuable service than she was doing.

Duncan Catling was the first American ever to live in Batu Pahat. Naturally he was the center of interest in the town. The teachers with whom he taught at the Boys' High School found an attractive house for him, cleaned it, and helped Duncan find furniture. As soon as his new neighbors discovered that Duncan was interested in gardening, they brought him plants.

Duncan's social life in Batu Pahat was as flourishing as his garden. He had many invitations to dinner, which permitted him to indulge his taste for Chinese, Indian, and Malay food. He attended dances at a club, enjoyed the local movies, had both adult friends and students at his house.

The boys' high school where Duncan taught English and literature had five forms and enrolled fourteen hundred students. The buildings were modern and attractive. The headmaster was progressive and hardworking. The school had both a sports and a club program. Duncan was pleased with the recent work of the Dramatics Club that had produced *Macbeth* for a four-nights' run, with the young volunteer acting as a codirector of the performance.

Duncan, an articulate and forthright young man, was critical of the prevailing system of instruction and testing. Like other volunteer teachers, he deplored the students' unwillingness to discuss or answer questions in class, and he thought that the syllabus for each of his courses needed to be changed.

A newly announced educational policy in Malaysia was praised by Duncan. Under one provision of the new policy, failure to pass examinations at the end of standard six (grade six) will no longer cause termination of a child's educational opportunities, as was formerly the case.

A new municipal library building in Johore Bahru was waiting to be equipped, staffed, and opened for use. When Rita Warpeha received the Peace Corps assignment to put a library into operation in this building, she was overjoyed.

When Rita joined the Peace Corps she was a trained librarian with one year's experience in a college library. In her new assignment she drew upon both training and experience, but she found that the job also called for initiative, ingenuity, and good judgment. Rita designed equipment and searched out materials for its construction. She bought and catalogued books. She selected and trained staff members.

The first books that Rita bought were in Malay and English. As funds permitted, she added books in Chinese and Tamil. The latter is a South Indian language used by some Malaysians.

Rita worked for the municipality of Johore Bahru. She soon discovered that an important part of her job was to help the municipal council members understand the purpose and function of a library. How well Rita succeeded in educating the council was shown at the dedication of the library ten months after her arrival in Johore Bahru. The library had equipment and books, four local staff members, and a budget for the next year four times the one for the first year.

When the Industrial Training Institute moved into a new building near Kuala Lumpur in early 1964, two Peace Corps volunteers were on its staff. A third volunteer soon arrived to join them.

The Institute was organized to improve the technical skills of boys apprenticed to trades. It was government-supported so students came from all over Malaysia. The Institute's program was set up in six terms of eight weeks each. To complete the course an apprentice spent one term each year for four years, while continuing to work at his apprenticeship in the intervening months. He was paid apprentice wages while attending the Institute.

The students at the Institute, ranging in age from sixteen to twenty-one, had usually not gone beyond standard six, the final year of primary school, or form one, the first year of secondary school. While the instruction was largely technical, it included the science and mathematics that were necessary for understanding and performing the technical work. Each instructor carried one group of boys through a term, working with them eight hours each day. He was responsible for both academic and shop work. The Institute provided a brief syllabus for each course, but the instructors had to supplement this.

Charles Donegan taught welding and machine shop. Frank Harrington was also a machine shop instructor. Alfred Chin taught air conditioning and refrigeration. The Institute had additional programs in bookbinding, printing, automotive repair, heat treating, electrical trades, and electronics.

Charles was an experienced machinist who had owned his

own shop for eleven years. He heard that the Peace Corps needed machinists, so he applied to the Corps. He had never had any teaching experience, but he found that he liked to teach when there was no language barrier between him and the students. His immediate problem was caused by three Chinese boys in his group who had no other language. Since Charles had no Chinese, an English-speaking Chinese boy interpreted. But, Charles asked, ruefully, "How do I give those boys a test?"

Frank Harrington worked for several years as a model maker at a Naval Ordinance Laboratory. He read in his union paper that machinists were needed in the Peace Corps. Frank applied to the Corps, but as he put it, "I was certainly surprised when I was selected." Like Charles, he found teaching interesting and rewarding.

Alfred Chin, a Chinese-American and a graduate in electrical engineering, had worked two and a half years as a development engineer before entering the Peace Corps. One day Alfred saw a film about Peace Corps work in South America. Telling of this, Alfred said, "That film planted a seed in my mind. I did not think that my job was very important, so after a time I filled out a Peace Corps application."

Alfred enjoyed teaching. However, he suspected that his greatest contribution was his presence in Malaysia, for it was hard for local people to believe that a man of Chinese ancestry was a full-fledged American.

A new coeducational institution, the Malayan Teachers College, was opened in 1962 at Kuala Lumpur. The College, which had a two-year program, admitted students who had finished form five with a good academic record, but preferred students who had completed form six. Two Peace Corps volunteers served this institution almost from its beginning.

Mary Holm taught literature and English as a second language at the College. She used lectures and discussion and gave assignments in both reading and writing. Since the college was new, Mary developed her own courses with help from the department head on book selection.

There were college clubs, societies, dances, and tours, which involved the teachers in sponsoring and chaperoning. Mary helped with a dramatics club. In this new college social contacts between men and women were permitted.

Mary Holm had a nice apartment in a dormitory, in which she served as a warden. She found congenial groups in Kuala Lumpur through which she made friends. Mary enjoyed her work and her personal life in Kuala Lumpur. Yet she said, "I think that someone else would have done what I have done, if I had not been here."

Kent Keeth, with a master's degree in library science, arrived in Kuala Lumpur when the Malayan Teachers College was nine months old. The opportunity for creative work was present in Kent's Peace Corps assignment to act as the college librarian. Added to this was the freedom that he was accorded to do, within the limits of the library budget, what he wanted to do to build up the library. The expanded, well-organized, much-used library that the college had two years later was a monument to Kent's wise use of his opportunities.

Kent got an extension of a few months in order to close his period of service at the end of a school term. He felt pride in his solid accomplishment, but he also harbored a strong sense of dissatisfaction because no counterpart had been assigned to be trained by him. He feared that the lack of a trained person to assume responsibility when he left would cause the library to lose much of its effectiveness. Kent was an ambitious, dynamic young man, whose natural desire to have the library continue led him to impatience with the factors that limited its growth and usefulness.

Each day seemed to have more hours after Ransom Townsend retired from teaching. He missed having boys around him, too. During the years that he taught architectural drawing in a city high school there was never a lack of boys and the days never had enough hours. The small, twinkly-eyed, ex-schoolmaster pondered the matter. One day he mentioned it to his wife Helen, who admitted that she too, had noticed that retirement brought changes.

Ransom Townsend began to read articles about the Peace Corps. He and Helen considered the possibility of enlisting in the Corps. They mentioned the matter to their three grown children who were co-operative, even if skeptical about such a course. After much thought, Ransom and Helen made application to join the Peace Corps. Nine months later, when the Townsends had concluded that nothing would come of the matter, they were accepted. After receiving training, which at times seemed strenuous for people in their sixties, they were sent to Malaysia to teach boys.

Ransom and Helen had between them more than sixty-three years of teaching experience. They had reared children and enjoyed grandchildren. At Technical Institute Secondary Boys' School in Kuala Lumpur, they did not feel in the least strange. Their students were boys, much like those they had always known, boys who needed to be guided and stimulated, prodded and praised.

Ransom taught architectural and technical drawing. Helen taught English. The course at the school covered three years, with the examinations which determined the students' future coming at the end of the third year. The Townsends discovered that this plan encouraged students to loaf for their first year or two and then cram furiously during the third year. The plan also led some students to think that learning was important only as a means of passing an examination.

During one term Helen spent four days reading a story to a class, with explanations and gestures to insure the boys' understanding of it. On the fifth day she gave a test on the story. A boy raised his hand and said, "I am unable to take this test."

"Why can't you take it?" Helen asked.

"You didn't tell us you were going to give a test, so I didn't listen," was the boy's candid reply.

Ransom and Helen lived in a four-room house on the campus. The house was lifted high on stilts in a style often found in Malay houses. Under Helen's touch the house became a home. The mosquito-net-hung beds were Malaysian, but the books on the shelves, the cookies in the jar, and the corn in the popper were pure American.

It seemed only natural to Helen to invite students to drop in to see them in their home. The boys were shy and well aware of the Malaysian custom that permitted no intimacy between students and teachers. But very soon the boys were visiting the Townsends. They came to borrow books, to receive extra help on their lessons, to sit quietly and read, to learn to pop corn, to devour cookies. They basked so fully in the friendly atmosphere generated by Helen's smiling enthusiasm and Ransom's kindly twinkle that the Townsends had to establish visiting hours. They let it be known that on four nights a week their home was open for two hours to their students.

The boys showed their appreciation of the Townsends' kindness. They aided Ransom and Helen's efforts to learn to eat with chopsticks. They brought native fruits and other small gifts when they came to visit. They invited Ransom and Helen to visit in their homes. Many undoubtedly shared the sentiment expressed by one boy when the time came for saying good-by.

Helen told her class that she and Ransom were leaving at the end of the term. Then she said, "I want you to come to see us when you come to America."

The boys thanked her but indicated that none was likely ever to go to America. Then one boy, perhaps sensing the true meaning of the Peace Corps, added, "But anyway it is good to know that *we* have someone in America."

Improving Physical Conditions

A small white-clad nurse pedaled along a dirt road in Malaysia. Beside the road ran a drainage ditch well filled with water from recent rains. A woman on the roadside called a cheery greeting which the nurse acknowledged with a friendly wave. The movement caused her to lose her balance on the bicycle. A moment later she rocketed head first into the drainage ditch.

The woman ran screaming toward the ditch. Her loud cries brought *kampong* (village) people to help fish a very bedraggled little nurse out of the muddy water. Her nurse's cap was gone, her dark hair hung in wisps, but she came up smiling.

Erin O'Brien, Peace Corps nurse newly arrived in Ayer Baloi, had been introduced to her neighbors. Recalling the manner of the introduction some time later, Erin said, "There couldn't have been a better way to break the ice. It made me appear very human."

As the months passed the small nurse was to become well known to the kampong people. Presiding over the maternal and child health program at the Health Subcenter in Ayer Baloi, Erin treated six to eight hundred patients each month. She gave the babies immunizations and gave their mothers advice on feeding and bathing them. It was on Erin's home visits, however, that the kampong people came to value fully the gentle touch and deep concern of the nurse for her small patients. Joking and chatting in fluent Malay, the nurse went into the houses where she was given a warm welcome. But when she took a little child on her lap and began to check his well-being, she was quietly serious and wholly competent, and the mothers gave her their full attention. The growing number of mothers who also followed her instructions testified to the acceptance that Erin had won from the kampong people.

Assisting Erin at the Subcenter in Ayer Baloi was a Malaysian nurse, a midwife, and an *amah*. The latter performed routine duties that in America would be done by nurses' aides. Expectant mothers received care at prenatal clinics held at the Subcenter. The midwife delivered babies in the homes, but Erin sometimes advised hospital deliveries for difficult cases.

Twice a week, Erin also served the Health Subcenter at Benut, making the eight-mile trip on her bicycle. She conducted a program there similar to the one at Ayer Baloi.

Erin taught a health class at Pontian for the local women. They wanted to learn to do complicated processes and it required all of Erin's tact to persuade them to learn instead simple first aid and health measures.

One day a Chinese boy confided to Erin his desire for an American pen pal. The nurse fulfilled his desire by enlisting the co-operation of her young brother. An international correspondence soon flourished and the Chinese boy proudly announced that he had a "foreign sister."

Erin lived alone in the nurses' house at the Subcenter in Ayer Baloi. Her hobby was learning to prepare Malaysian and Chinese food. The townspeople dropped by to visit. The people in the kampong scattered among the pineapple and rubber plantations kept a watchful eye on the young nurse. Erin was not lonely because she was surrounded by friends.

Malaysia has some private hospitals and doctors in private practice, but there is also a government health service, paid for by the federal government and administered by the states. In each state there is one general hospital. In each of the several districts within a state there is a district hospital. The hospitals handle much of the medical and all of the surgical treatments.

To provide facilities for the rural, or kampong, people, there is a network of rural health centers and subcenters. Each center is usually headed by a doctor who has a staff of nurses and other health workers assisting him. There are subcenters, often five in number, administered by each center. A subcenter usually has a staff nurse or other trained worker who handles general out-patient cases. It also has a nurse who has charge of a maternal and child care program. The plan also calls for maternal, or midwife, subcenters around each health subcenter, but these last are not yet fully in operation. Rural patients who need hospital care are sent to a district hospital. The emphasis in the rural centers and subcenters is upon developing good health practices, with strong emphasis upon maternal and child health. Patients do not pay for service received at the centers and subcenters, but all except those requiring charity pay for hospital care.

Erin O'Brien headed the maternal and child health service in a rural subcenter. Most of the Peace Corps nurses working in Malaysia had similar assignments. Their duties varied somewhat, but they usually included holding clinics for expectant mothers and for babies, giving immunizations, teaching good health practices, advising hospitalizations for those who needed a physician, and through patient and repeated explanation spreading understanding about such factors as sanitation and nutrition. In all of these activities the first need was to build a friendly relationship so that the people would have confidence in the nurse and accept her health teaching. As one Peace Corps nurse said, "Small talk comes before health talk."

Mary Ann Lawrie was the Peace Corps nurse in charge of maternal and child care at Sri Menanti Rural Health Subcenter. Mary Ann, usually known by her nickname, Toni, was aided in her work with the mothers and babies by an assistant nurse, a midwife, a student midwife, and an amah. A male staff nurse was in charge of general out-patient care at the subcenter.

The subcenter at Sri Menanti, like most of those in the rural health system, was housed in a small modern building designed for the purpose it served. The standard living quarters provided in the system were comfortable and adequate. Toni's house had a living room, dining room, two bedrooms, a storeroom, and a kitchen, with bath and toilet facilities on the walled patio.

Like Erin, Toni served in a second subcenter. She spent two days a week at each subcenter and two days in home visits.

Peace Corps volunteers are warned during training that they may suffer culture shock, a state of mind caused by the sharp contrast between the environment that the volunteer has always known and his new environment. Not all volunteers experience culture shock, but Toni Lawrie did.

Toni survived the period of acute shock, but as she went about her work she was troubled by some of the factors affecting health in Malaysia. She found it difficult to adjust to the British system of nursing, which makes nursing duties largely supervisory. Toni was irked by what she considered an over-emphasis upon status. She felt that there was a need for more democracy in human relationships.

The need for repeated teaching of even the simplest principles of health sometimes tried Toni's patience. But, realizing the need for health education, Toni said again and again, often to the same mother, "You must not give the baby ditch water." By patient repetition of this warning and of many health rules Toni laid the foundation for better health in Sri Menanti.

The government health services in Malaysia include leprosariums to care for patients suffering with leprosy. Hildur Johnson was the fourth Peace Corps nurse to serve at Sungei Buloh Settlement, the largest institution of its type in Malaysia.

The hospital at Sungei Buloh cares for three to four hundred patients. After a patient's leprosy is past the active stage he is discharged from the hospital to quarters in the settlement. If he improves sufficiently he may be discharged entirely. However, some patients who have been badly scarred by the disease choose to remain at the settlement, which is their privilege.

The recovered or partly recovered patients do bedside nurs-

ing and all the maintenance work in the hospital and the settlement, which occupies a large tract of land. They care for
themselves entirely, take part in settlement activities, and elect
members to the council which governs the settlement.

Hildur Johnson worked in the unit of the hospital where research was done on certain selected cases. Her duties were to
supervise the bedside care of the patients and to keep records.
The research unit had usually fifty to sixty patients.

Hildur's duties were not unique because she was in a lepro-
sarium, but she found the work interesting. She soon discovered
that the leprosy patients were sensitive to anyone having an
aversion to them because of their ailment and deeply appreciative of the nurse who did not have.

The cause of leprosy is a bacillus but how it is transmitted
from person to person is not known. Asked what the nurses did
to protect themselves, Hildur said, "Nothing beyond normal
sanitary practices."

Once a month Hildur went with a doctor to a fishing village
on a small island off the coast. Hildur assisted the doctor as he
examined the people. It was a rare trip that did not produce
new cases. Why this village is so afflicted with leprosy is one
of the mysteries that may be unraveled when the means of
transmitting the disease is established.

Hildur Johnson is a mature woman. She has two grown children and seven grandchildren. Hildur believed that a volunteer
had to win the confidence of his co-workers before he could
teach them new techniques. She thought that the process of
winning confidence sometimes began with learning upon the
part of the volunteer. Of this problem, Hildur said, "I have
learned much here and discovered that I don't know it all.
There are many ways of doing things."

Rosemarie Joswick was a laboratory technician assigned to
the General Hospital in Seremban. This was the largest and
most important hospital in the state. Rosemarie was the only

woman technician in a laboratory with ten or twelve male technicians. She had had seven years' experience and she was eager
to be of service, but she was not given a full schedule until she
had proved her competence. After her position in the laboratory
was established, Rosemarie was happy in the assignment. However, she questioned whether there might not be greater need
for her services in a hospital less well staffed than the one where
she was assigned.

Rosemarie was uncomfortable because she was not fulfilling
the Peace Corps "image." She lived in pleasant quarters in the
nurses' hostel and had an interesting social life. She said, "I am
having such a good time that I feel guilty. I hope I can be
placed in a job that requires more sacrifice on my part."

There are about fifty thousand aborigines in Malaya. They
are descendants of very early people who wandered down the
peninsula and found living space in the jungle. The aborigines
still retain their own languages and habits of living. Some of
them live entirely off the jungle, others hack out small openings
and raise food crops. Some have a few chickens. They fish and
hunt wild boar. They are industrious, if there is work to do.
Some find jobs tapping rubber trees.

In recent years concern about providing health services for
the aborigines led to the establishment of Rumah Sakit Orang
Asli. This institution is commonly called the Aborigine Hospital, though it is considered by the government to be a re-
habilitation center. It is located at Gombak, twelve miles from
Kuala Lumpur.

The Aborigine Hospital, under the direction of Dr. Malcolm
Bolton, draws patients from all over the country. It has eight
detached wards for general care as well as maternity wards that
provide both prenatal and postnatal care. There are living
quarters, because a patient who goes to the hospital is always
accompanied by someone in his family and often by the whole
family. The relatives cook for the patient and keep him com-

pany. They swarm about the hospital grounds, the women wearing sarongs knotted at the waist, the men in pajamalike garments. Each mother carries her baby in a cloth tied over her shoulder. Men, women, and children smoke. A woman often carries an extra cigarette in her pierced ear lobe. The hospital is always crowded. With facilities for 150 it often shelters three hundred persons.

Aborigines have a poor diet. Many are infected with parasites. The hospital at Gombak has a large number of tubercular patients. Dr. Bolton and his staff strive not only to cure immediate ailments but to teach the aborigines to eat a proper diet, to practice sanitation, and to observe other health rules.

Health services are provided in the areas where the aborigines live by forty medical posts, each manned by an aborigine who has had a few weeks of training in health practices. He attends to simple ailments and notifies the hospital by wireless of severe illnesses. The patient is then picked up by truck or helicopter and taken to the hospital.

The Aborigine Hospital is partly staffed by service agencies. In 1964 CARE had a doctor and two nurses on duty. At the same time the Peace Corps had a doctor, two nurses, and a teacher serving at the hospital.

Dr. Elizabeth Cole was a retired physician when she joined the Peace Corps, but she was far from retired during her tour of duty at the Aborigine Hospital. As part of her work Dr. Cole traveled by Land Rover to certain of the medical posts and to the kampongs around them. On these trips Dr. Cole examined the local people and treated those who were ill. She took patients who needed to go to the hospital in the Land Rover or wired from the medical post for the hospital to send a helicopter. Dr. Cole spent about half of her time in jungle practice.

Marilyn Haasnoot, a Peace Corps volunteer, was the only nurse at the Aborigine Hospital for the first year of her service there. She set up the maternity unit, which included prenatal, postnatal, and delivery areas. Marilyn delivered the babies at the maternity unit until aborigine women were trained to do so. Marilyn, and later the other nurses, held prenatal clinics once a week for expectant mothers and provided postnatal care for those who had recently had babies. Marilyn also supervised bedside nursing in other wards and assisted with immunizations given to patients to protect against a number of diseases.

Marilyn participated in work in the jungle fringes beyond the area served by the medical posts. She and another nurse went out at intervals on one-day trips. On each trip they went to some central point in the kampong visited and spread the news by word of mouth that they were there. When the people came, the nurses immunized, applied dressings, and tried to persuade the seriously sick to go to the Aborigine Hospital.

Marilyn had a satisfying experience. She worked with good doctors and appreciative patients in a situation in which she had some authority—a happy combination of circumstances.

Robert Corbin was trained as a nurse before he joined the Peace Corps. At the Aborigine Hospital he gave immunizations and did tuberculosis testing. He hoped also to train an aborigine to perform these skilled functions. Because the hospital needed a laboratory technician with a full range of technical skills, Robert took training in Kuala Lumpur to meet this need.

Soon after Robert arrived he went with Dr. Bolton on a five-day trip into the jungle. The men carried air mattresses, food, a small stove, a kettle, and mosquito repellent, in addition to medicines and dressings. They slept in the native kampongs, prepared their food, and boiled their water. They traveled on the rivers with an aborigine guide, using either a motorboat or a canoe. Dr. Bolton dispensed medical services wherever the men went.

The doctor was much concerned with reaching all the aborigines. At intervals he went by helicopter to the most remote areas occupied by these people. He also set up plans for Robert to work out of the medical posts to carry immunization and certain other services to the people in the jungle. Robert was highly pleased that he was to have a part in this program.

There were many children among the families receiving treatment at the Aborigine Hospital. The Peace Corps assigned Susan Mapes to teach the aborigine children at the hospital.

Susan described her school as a "catch-as-catch-can" project. Most of the children spoke only in an aborigine tongue and many could not read or write. Susan tried to keep reviewed the facts that the children who had been to school knew. She worked with pre-school materials to build a readiness to learn in those children who had had no opportunity to attend school. The schoolroom where Susan worked was a gloomy place with little equipment, but the hospital supplied books, paper, pencils, and crayons as these were needed.

The young volunteer was trained in speech correction. She was classified on hospital records as an occupational therapist, a position for which she had no direct training. She did, however, perform certain practical functions in this field, buying supplies needed for projects and giving supervision and encouragement to them. Under Susan's watchful eye two crippled aborigines wove baskets, the men made sun blinds, and the children pasted scrapbooks for the amusement of bed patients. With some additional guidance from other sources, the women sewed blouses and baby shirts. Susan tutored certain children recommended by the doctor for this extra help. The changing and informal nature of her assignment led Susan to say, "It is hard for me to see what I have accomplished." She added hopefully, "But I believe I have helped some."

A path like a green tunnel led deep into the Malaysian jungle. A small party, headed by William Null, a Peace Corps volunteer, moved along the path. Behind Bill walked four Malaysians, each carrying a big metal box. A crashing sound ahead brought the men to a sudden halt, just as an elephant came out of the jungle onto the cleared path. Behind him a second elephant appeared, then a third, a fourth, and finally a fifth animal crashed through the undergrowth of the jungle onto the path.

The minute the animals came into view the bearers dropped their metal boxes. Grabbing sticks, they danced around the boxes pounding them vigorously and at the same time yelling like maniacs. The startled elephants stood their ground for a minute or two, then as the pandemonium continued, the giant beasts turned tail and lumbered off down the path.

Bill Null was a Peace Corps volunteer assigned to work as a soil surveyor in Johore, a state in Malaysia. He worked under the direction of the Ministry of Agriculture. It was Bill's job to secure and analyze samples of soil to test its fertility. In order to get into the jungle-covered area assigned to him, Bill had paths cut every two and a half miles. The paths led from main roads into the jungle. On each trip Bill and the four bearers who carried supplies stayed seven days, camping each night beside a stream. After being delivered to their area of work in a truck, the men made their way down a path, with Bill making a soil boring every quarter of a mile to secure a sample.

The jungle sheltered animal life ranging from chiggers to elephants. The men saw tracks of wild oxen and signs of many other jungle creatures. One morning Bill awoke to find tiger tracks a few feet from his sleeping place. But in two years of tramping jungle paths and camping beside the streams Bill and his bearers suffered no more serious injuries than those inflicted by chiggers, ticks, and leeches.

When Bill's two-year tour of duty ended, he had not finished surveying the two and a half million acres of jungle assigned to him. Bill found working in the jungle monotonous, but he asked for a six months extension in order to finish the job. The extension was granted and the survey was completed.

Bill's decision to extend was influenced by the action of a group of nationals from another country. These men also had an assignment that was not completed when their period of service ended. The men left and the project upon which they had worked collapsed. This situation led Bill to feel that more than the completion of soil testing was involved. As Bill put it, "I decided I had to finish my assignment. I wanted Americans to complete, not quit, what they undertook."

Malaysia has a program for rural development. One aspect of the program is sponsored by a government agency known as the Federal Land Development Authority. The purpose of this agency is to secure the clearing and planting of selected jungle areas, the settlement of people in such areas, and the develop-

Don Moseley works on a land development project which clears land and establishes settlements near Jasin, Malaysia.

ment of normal community life among the settlers. Several volunteers have served in these land development projects.

The work on such a project begins with the selection of a site suitable for settlement. Timber having commercial value is removed, after which the other jungle growth is cut down and burned and the land is planted. Rubber has proved to be well adapted to the type of operation carried out by the Land Development Authority.

The settlers provide the labor needed to turn the jungle into a functioning community. They are paid wages for their work, but they are also earning a more substantial share in the economy of the community. At the end of a fixed period they receive a tract of productive land as their own.

Don Moseley worked in a project sponsored by the Federal Land Development Authority a few miles from Jasin. Settlers had already established a community when Don arrived. He was not assigned a specific job, but was expected to be useful in ways dictated by the needs of the community.

Don soon found two principal avenues of activity, as well as scores of specific tasks that needed willing hands. In all the development communities there is a need to foster undertakings that will provide the settlers a supplement to their diet and some income beyond their wages. Don helped to establish six fishponds which were expected to produce ten tons of fish per year. The project was organized as a production and marketing co-operative. The settlers who wished to have a part in the co-operative paid a monthly subscription rate and shared in the profits of the enterprise. Don secured nine rabbits and started the production of breeding stock for settlers who wanted to raise rabbits. He kept a flock of chickens and produced eggs which settlers could use to hatch chicks.

The community needed a recreational program and Don attacked this need with enthusiasm. His plan for building interest in a particular sport or game was to organize a council of citizens to promote and support it. When he had several such councils operating he organized them into an over-all sports council. Naturally these activities led to the need for playing fields and a recreation building and Don was soon co-ordinating the work of securing these. Under his guidance the boys and men of the community rebuilt an old barracks into a recreation hall. With some financial assistance from the government, two soccer fields were prepared.

The land development scheme in Bilut Valley near Bentong covers fifty-seven hundred acres, or about nine square miles. The settlers were carefully selected and recruited from all parts of the country. They included Malays, Chinese, and Indians. In 1959, when the scheme received its first settlers, 328 families went to Bilut Valley. Other settlers followed. At the end of 1964 there were about six hundred families and some forty-two hundred people in the community. Each family lived in its own house and had a three-acre tract upon which the family could plant an orchard and garden and raise animals for food.

The community had a primary school with instruction in the morning in Malay and in the afternoon in Chinese, Tamil, and English. The school enrolled 650 children and had twenty-six teachers. The community had both a mosque and a church.

After the land was cleared it was planted with hybrid rubber seedlings. The settlers cared for the rubber plantations under supervision. Rubber comes into production after seven years of growth. By the time the trees in Bilut Valley are in production the settlers will probably have completed the organization of a marketing co-operative. By selling to a processing plant which produces the type of liquid latex desired by factories abroad the rubber growers can increase their profits.

When a settler has met the required conditions he will receive seven acres of the land under rubber, three acres of orchard and garden land, and his homesite. Because of the high yield of rubber trees seven acres will provide a reasonable income.

John Shay was a chemical engineer working with rubber and plastics in a large manufacturing concern. He wanted to see the great rubber plantations whose product he used and he was interested in people. These motives led him to join the Peace Corps and he was assigned to work at Bilut Valley.

John was given two specific directives. He was to work under the manager of the Development Scheme in carrying out certain administrative matters and he was to establish small-project activities to improve nutrition and increase income.

One of the administrative matters on which John gave help was the education of the workers concerning the care of rubber plantings. He was especially concerned with the eradication of the lalang weed and of certain diseases that menaced rubber production. John used films and found the men interested and responsive to the instruction.

In following his second directive John promoted the establishment of fish ponds. Thirteen ponds were built by individual owners. In one case five friends pooled their efforts and made a large pond that they owned jointly. The ponds were all located near streams. Building a pond involved digging a depression and erecting a dam to hold the water which was carried by pipes from the stream into the depression. Each pond had a drain so that it could be emptied and cleaned at intervals. The ponds were fertilized to stimulate plant growth which provided food for the fish. The owners secured stock for their ponds from the federal fisheries and fed the young fish for several weeks. The fish ponds came into production in eight months and yielded a good harvest. A nearby town provided a market for the surplus fish.

John performed many functions in the fish-pond project. He attended a four-day training session at a government hatchery to secure information. He organized a trip made by a group of the settlers at Bilut Valley to a fish-breeding station. He explained the profits to be made from a pond. He directed construction of the ponds and helped the owners to operate them effectively. And while he taught the people useful techniques, he also taught them self-reliance.

John, a dynamo of energy, found time to work with the local veterinarian in upgrading chickens and launching controlled poultry projects. He coached the local soccer team and took an interest in various other community activities.

When we were leaving Bilut Valley, John said to us, "I have discovered that these people have the same hopes and desires that Americans have."

John Shay had touched on a general truth. Around the world millions of people have the same hopes and desires that Americans have. To help them learn how to realize their hopes and fulfill their desires through their own efforts is the mission of the American Peace Corps.

Summing Up

Our journey to three continents ended. We returned home, to sort out the impressions that flooded our minds and to bring into focus the meaning to be gained from our pilgrimage to see the Peace Corps in action.

When we reviewed the happenings we had seen and the conversations we had held the real significance of the Peace Corps became clear to us. The Peace Corps is evidence, for all the world to see, that America cares about the world's disadvantaged people. To express this concern in practical ways the Peace Corps program teaches skills, spreads understanding, and develops self-reliance. The Peace Corps volunteer at his best kindles the spark which at full blaze destroys illness and ignorance, prejudice and poverty.

Index